LOVE WORTHY

21 Lessons in Creating a Deliciously Divine Life

Jo Worthy

LOVE WORTHY: 21 Lessons in Creating a Deliciously Divine Life
© JO WORTHY 2019

The moral rights of Jo Worthy to be identified as the author of this work have been asserted in accordance with the Copyright Act 1968

First published in Australia 2019 by Jo Worthy

www.joworthy.com

ISBN 978-0-6485885-8-0

All rights reserved. No part of this publication may be reproduced or transmitted by any means, electronic, photocopying or otherwise, without prior written permission of the author.

Disclaimer

Any opinions expressed in this work are exclusively those of the author and are not necessarily the views held or endorsed by the publisher. All the information, techniques, skills and concepts contained within this publication are of the nature of general comment only, and are not in any way recommended as individual advice. The intent is to offer a variety of information to provide a wider range of choices now and in the future, recognising that we all have widely diverse circumstances and viewpoints. Should any reader choose to make use of the information herein, it is their decision, and the author and publisher/s do not assume any responsibilities whatsoever under any conditions or circumstances. The author does not take responsibility for the business, financial, personal or other success, results or fulfilment upon the readers' decision to use this information. It is recommended that the reader obtain their own independent advice.

This book is dedicated to every woman who has experienced low self-worth and a lack of self-love. For every woman who has been through deep sorrow and suffering associated with their poor judgement, particularly related to their relationship choices. For every woman who thinks they are not good enough and for every woman who does not honour herself, or is struggling to connect with their own unique beautiful essence. I understand you, I feel you, and I support and honour your own personal journey.

From my heart to yours, I would love for you to create a life that is extraordinary, one that is "Magnificent". A life that exceeds your expectations, and one that you know deep down to your very core that you are deserving of and that you feel exceptionally Love Worthy.

May you find love, be loved, and live a life that is passionate and purposeful.

"The woman in ME celebrates and honours the woman in YOU".

Much Love & Abundance
Jo Worthy

Foreword

Hello dear reader,

My name is Steffanie Jean and I am the daughter of Jo Worthy. It is my absolute honour to tell you about the exceptional woman that I call my mum.

I want to share with you the journey I have experienced with my mother since my birth in 1993 and what I remember growing up and also now as a young woman.

I want this piece to be a tribute to honour my mother and to let you know how I am particularly proud of the fact that she has endured so much yet triumphed and achieved so much in the past 26 years of my life. There are many reasons why I admire my mum.

I want to express to you that my mum has always had the ability to show compassion and the capacity to love and display such kindness and generosity. I also feel that my mum is one of the most hospitable people that I know. She welcomes all to her home and was never judgmental.

I was fortunate that my mum always supported my choices and dreams. She would always encourage me to follow my heart and to always do the best that I could under any circumstances. She didn't put any undue expectations or pressure upon me and embraced my individuality. My mum's motto was always to *"use honey not vinegar"* when communicating and dealing with others.

It is evident at times that we both didn't live an easy life and we suffered emotional pain. However, looking back as young adult now, sometimes I am quite amazed how she continued to raise me with such love considering the challenges that she was dealing with. My mum became a single mum when I was 3, and she had to "dig deep" and learn to survive and continue on her path without knowing what was coming next. I want to express to you that she did a damn good job!

We did move houses on several occasions and to different suburbs, although once I got to school age, Mum had my very best interests at heart and because she wanted a good education for me we moved a few times so I could attend schools with better reputations.

What I also love and appreciate about my Mum is that she also wanted to make sure that she created a beautiful home for us. I also felt very lucky that she was a great cook and was passionate about food. I always remember Mum going to the markets and buying such fresh produce and many times organic even when she must have been on a tight budget.

Mum also encouraged good manners and even though she was not overly strict, she would make sure that I treated others respectfully and with kindness. I loved that she supported my dreams and encouraged my hobbies and other creative pursuits. She always wanted the BEST for me and she worked hard to make sure I didn't miss out on some luxuries.

I really wanted to express that I admire my Mum's spirit so much and that she is so resilient and courageous, similar to a *"Phoenix rising from the Ashes"*. I say this because I have witnessed that no matter what comes her way, no matter when she falls down, or faced some of her biggest fears, she always got back up again and did everything within her power to create a better life for herself and her loved ones, including myself.

She has also been such a great role-model in regards to natural healing and soothing her own soul and to also help me, including being so generous with paying for alternative therapies for me as well. She has amazed me with her strength and that she always comes back from adversity stronger, better and much wiser and has taught me some valuable life lessons in these regards.

I also love the fact that my Mum genuinely loves other people succeeding in life and that she has a pure loving heart. I have witnessed her helping others many times and that her ability to see the good in others and any situation is admirable. I remember that my mother has always been quite intuitive and has a great passion and knowledge for astrology. She has an innate ability to guide and mentor people that cross her path and I have seen others seek her guidance frequently.

I was so emotional writing this because it made me reflect more deeply on how much my mother means to me. To see her write this book, follow her dreams and know and feel deeply that she is such a good woman, I am really so very proud to be her daughter. For mum to be able to share her lessons and her journey to you all is beyond incredible.

I think my mum simply is a powerhouse, and that she has really has set the tone and will influence many more generations to come for the betterment of all who cross her path and they will certainly be blessed.

I am truly honoured and so grateful to have Jo Worthy as my mum. Mum, I love you and thank you for being you!

With love - Steffanie Jean

Preface

Writing this book has been a huge project. Many times, I questioned whether I would finish it and if it would ever be published. I would experience moments of self-doubt and fear, and think: who am I kidding that I could help others with my story? Would other women connect with me? Would my book even be inspiring?

I took writing this book very seriously, and it was never going to be a project that could ever be rushed. I recognised I had to put my entire heart and soul into writing it, otherwise it wouldn't be worthwhile publishing. I certainly wanted my readers to not only find my book enjoyable, inspiring, and entertaining, I also wanted it to be a reference to help others on their own journeys.

This is a very raw and honest account of my life, so there were many times I feared judgement, criticism, and exposure. I wasn't sure whether I should publish it, because it is so revealing. I had already started to feel so exposed and naked prior to being published.

Now that the book is in your hands, you can see I kept on going and you can now read about my life, my joy, my pain, and the enormous journey I have experienced. I had to dig deep at times to persevere, as it took a lot of courage, discipline, and resilience to get it published. It also needed inspiration from my mentors and supporters who continued to encourage me along the way.

Whenever I felt like I couldn't keep going, I would go back to my "why". Revealing my story was not just about my own healing journey. Even though it was a huge release to be able to, I didn't want to write a book solely for this reason. I knew that my readers needed and deserved more than just a healing release for me. I wanted this book to be of benefit and inspiration to the reader.

I have witnessed and read about many women who suffer from their pasts. These women are holding onto childhood pain, teenage memories of bullying, feeling worthless, rejecting love and attracting abusive relationships, ultimately manifesting in low self-worth and self-love.

This is the biggest "why" for writing and publishing this book. If other people can relate to my story, they will find comfort in knowing they are not alone and there are other women experiencing similar suffering and emotions, and they can also decide to live a life of passion, joy and LOVE.

I felt that my story had to be told so that I could help other women to honour, believe in, and love themselves as well. I hope my story will inspire women to create their own magnificently abundant lives. This is why I finished this book, and I put my doubts and fears of exposure and judgment aside, hoping that it could make a difference to others.

Admittedly, my story is a huge one. At times it is very intense, to the point I even worried if it was too much. I would ask myself: will my readers just think "oh my goodness, this woman lives a life of drama and pain, but big deal and who even cares about her story?".

The real essence of this book is how I am now not only a survivor, but a woman who is starting to thrive. That is what I wish for you, and what I want to help you achieve throughout these pages.

I also thought that the courage of revealing my story would show you I am a living example of what is possible when you connect to your beautiful essence within your own true magnificence. You can transform from a caterpillar to a beautiful butterfly. You can rise above any challenges or pain that you may have experienced.

I know there may be some judgement regarding my behaviours, and the decisions I have made in my life will be questionable, but this also gives other women permission to own all parts of themselves — the good, the bad, and sometimes ugly – our shadow and our light.

If your self-worth and self-love practices are non-existent, you will most likely feel disillusioned, disconnected and "stuck". The good news is that you can choose to change, including changing your mindset and have higher expectations for your life. Make the decision right now to start believing more in YOU and do not accept anything but the BEST FOR YOU.

When we start setting a strong intention of abundance we can really start to manifest at a much higher vibration. The universe is waiting for you to be the very best version of yourself. So, it's time for you to stand in your own power within and claim it.

As I was in the middle of revising this manuscript, I listened to a talk by Brené Brown. It was no coincidence that I listened to her in this very sensitive moment of my writing process as some of her quotes were exactly what I needed to hear. The following is one that I loved:

"If you are not in the arena also getting your arse kicked, I am not interested in your feedback" – Brene Brown.

These words were so timely, as they related to my fears in telling my own story and the feedback I might receive from others. I realised that, unless those others are also being courageous and vulnerable, their judgments and criticisms would not count.

I sincerely hope, from the bottom of my heart, you enjoy reading my book and find it inspiring and insightful.

Table of Contents

Foreword vii
Preface xi
Introduction 1

Lesson 1
You are worthy of CREATIVITY 7
Your path to CREATIVITY 12

Lesson 2
You are worthy of being ADORED 21
Your path to ADORATION 26

Lesson 3
You are worthy of PLEASURE 33
Your path to PLEASURE 37

Lesson 4
You are worthy of HEALING 45
Your path to HEALING 50

Lesson 5
You are worthy of creating BOUNDARIES 57
Your path to creating BOUNDARIES 62

Lesson 6
You are worthy of OPULENCE 69
Your path to OPULENCE 74

Lesson 7
You are worthy of TRUTH 81
Your path to TRUTH 86

Lesson 8
You are worthy of FORGIVENESS 93
Your path to FORGIVENESS 99

Lesson 9
You are worthy of STABILITY 107
Your path to STABILITY 113

Lesson 10
You are worthy of ABUNDANCE 121
Your path to ABUNDANCE 128

Lesson 11
You are worthy of BLISS 139
Your Path to BLISS 145

Lesson 12
You are worthy of HARMONY 153
Your path to HARMONY 159

Lesson 13
You are worthy of FINDING LOVE AGAIN 167
Your Path to FINDING LOVE AGAIN 172

Lesson 14
You are worthy of FRIENDSHIP 181
Your path to FRIENDSHIP 187

Lesson 15
You are worthy of COMMUNITY 193
Your path to COMMUNITY 198

Lesson 16
You are worthy of living PASSIONATELY & ON PURPOSE 205
Your path to living PASSIONATELY & ON PURPOSE 211

Lesson 17
You are worthy of SURRENDERING 219
Your path to SURRENDERING 224

Lesson 18
You are worthy of UNCONDITIONAL LOVE 231
Your path to UNCONDITIONAL LOVE 237

Lesson 19
You are worthy of COMMITMENT 245
Your path to COMMITMENT 250

Lesson 20
You are worthy of MAGNIFICENCE 259
Your path to MAGNIFICENCE 261

Lesson 21
You are worthy of DREAMS COMING TRUE 273
Your Path to DREAMS COMING TRUE 277

Conclusion 283
Acknowledgments 287
About the Author 291
Sales Page 293

Introduction

Hello divine woman,

I wrote this book to help you reclaim the amazing power within you, and to help you to create your very own magnificent life. A life which you truly deserve, and one that you have desired and dreamed about. It's now time to realise that you can make your dreams a reality. It is **your time** to set a clear intention and connect to your magnificence.

This book shares 21 lessons to help guide you on your own personal journey of healing. My wish is that you love yourself more abundantly, so that every day of your life is overflowing with deeper meaning, joy, happiness, peace and of course, lots of love. These feelings are your birthright: it's like your soul is crying out for all of this and so much more. Please **believe** in yourself and know that you were you born to be **magnificent** and, under no circumstances, should you settle for mediocrity.

The purpose of sharing my story is to show you I have been there, in the darkest places, and to share with you that I have come back to the light as a wiser, happier, vibrant, and more loving woman. This is what I wish for you: **to live a deliciously divine life, one that sets your heart and soul on fire. I want you to believe that you are deserving of exactly this!**

I truly hope my book brings you insights into some of the challenges you may have had in the past, or that you may be experiencing right now. The biggest insight I hope you understand is, regardless of what you have experienced, you can return to your true path: the path of love. This is the path that you are mostly definitely worthy and deserving of, and the one you must give yourself permission to pursue.

I hope you can relate to at least some of my stories. I don't realistically think you are going to relate to all of them; however, you will relate to many of the feelings we both have shared. These feelings may include hopelessness, loneliness, loss, betrayal, and that horrible pit in your stomach with constant self-questioning of your own worth, leading to a perpetual attitude throughout your life of thinking you are not good enough.

My wish is the "lessons" I have outlined will make a difference in helping you to improve your own life. I also hope my story and lessons will provide inspiration to help you realise, regardless of any trauma or challenges you may have faced in the past, or are currently facing in your present, that now is the time for you to **create your own magnificent life**. It is time to dig deep within you to be the very best version of you. **It is time to make sure that you never give up on yourself or on love and most importantly your love for yourself.**

Have you lacked judgment and had difficulty creating solid boundaries which are most likely from your own lack of self-love and self-worth? If so, I can really relate to you and your suffering. Based on my personal experiences, believe me when I say **you can move on from the past and that you can create healthier boundaries and increase your own worth.**

If your life is not where you would like it to be, do not waste time blaming your family, ex-boyfriend, ex-partner, ex-husband or friends. You are the master of your destiny. You can choose to be happy, you can make choices that make you sing with delight, and you can choose the people to share all this magnificence with.

You can step into your **power**, use your **inner-wisdom**, connect to your inner-warrior goddess, so that you are shining your amazingness to the world and creating a life that is truly incredible. We ALL have that power within us, but you first need to start believing in YOU!

For me, there were many days when I couldn't see this, and I would momentarily accept my bland average life. I experienced some very dark days; days where I just numbed myself out because the emotional pain was too intense to even contemplate dealing with it consciously.

One of my biggest problems was I suffered from a huge lack of self-love. I didn't believe in *me,* and felt it so damn challenging to support myself. In turn, I didn't honour the true essence of who I was and all I could offer to the world. I also believe this is the reason I attracted some very toxic and abusive relationships. There were times in my life I was able to connect to my conscious thoughts, and it was in these moments I realised I was living a very mediocre, sad, and unstable existence. I did start to think "surely there is more to life"?

My life has been a rich tapestry of experiences; some tragic, some wonderful, and everything in between. It has included a dysfunctional childhood, filled with fears and insecurities, love I rejected, mental breakdowns, addictions, and numerous abusive and toxic relationships. Luckily, even on my darkest days, I never completely gave up. Believe me, it was a challenge at times, but I could see some light, I searched for more meaning and love, and I didn't completely give up on myself.

I have experienced financial ruin, and vast and various intimate relationships. I avoided my pain and inner torment with gambling and other forms of addiction, including sex, shopping, and food. I have been to the brink of disaster many times and come back like a phoenix rising from the ashes. I am a Scorpio sun sign after all, and in true "Scorpio" style, my lessons have been extremely transformational and through personal experience I can also help you with your transformations.

I hope my personal story is proof you can heal from the past, you can learn to trust again, you can fall in love and live the life you always imagined. Trusting in myself and working on my personal development, has been an absolutely cherished investment. To honour, to believe in, and to love myself have been the vital components to creating my extraordinary life, which led me to fall in love once again, and then to finally open my heart up entirely, to trust and love and commit myself fully to my man. May 2017 was an extremely special moment and a huge celebration, as I married my Mr. Worthy!

It took a lot of dedication to create the life I now have, and to become the woman I am today. I had to dig deep within and connect with my **courage, honesty, and vulnerability**. I had to become **totally conscious**, and deal with my challenges instead of avoiding them. Once I **opened up to even more healing**, I knew it would be deeper and far more powerful. A Healer once said to me *"What is revealed can be healed"*. These are my key components for you to utilise as well.

After so many years of self-doubts, fears, low self-worth, many toxic relationships, and some abusive relationships, I finally acknowledged: *enough was enough*. I was done with the life I had created, and I knew I needed to consciously change my ways. I am sure I was a bit insane at times, as I kept making the same mistakes and expecting a different result.

Fast forward to 2019, and my life in so many ways is completely different. I can honestly say I am now very proud I am well on the way to fully connecting with my own "magnificence". I now want you to celebrate your courage and resilience and be proud that you have overcome so much adversity. I want you to genuinely celebrate and honour the woman YOU have become. It may be quite a journey, but when you really start to believe in yourself, and connect to your true inner-beauty and zones of genius, watch how your life will change in amazing ways.

Divine woman, I **want you to connect with all your array of beautiful gifts, your "gold", your very own "genius" and your own worth.** I would love for you to allow yourself to shine your light brightly, and not dim yourself down to please or fit in with others. To stop being a **people-pleaser** and a **perfectionist** so you can truly spread your wings and fly to new heights.

Once you start to honour who you are and realise its time to start living the life YOU deserve, your life will begin to change in miraculous ways. I want you to be proud of what you have done to overcome your own challenges and to start living a fabulous life, not one filled with sadness, regret, shame or isolation, but **love, joy, peace and passion**. You need to decide that you do not have to keep suffering

My wish is you find my journey inspirational as I outline my key 21 lessons to create a "deliciously divine" life. My lessons reflect how I opened my eyes wide to allow myself to **heal, forgive and love**. My main message throughout my book is very clear, and that is to understand no matter what you have endured in your life, you can break the old destructive patterns, you can change your life to be the way you want it to be, and you can create your very own delicious life.

Here is a great affirmation for you:

> ***I am LOVE WORTHY and I live a deliciously divine and a magnificent life***

Much love,

Jo Worthy

"Creativity is contagious, pass it on"
— Albert Einstein

Lesson 1
You are Worthy of Creativity

I was born in 1964, and for the first 11 years of my life I grew up in a house in the north-eastern suburbs of Melbourne (Australia), with my mother, father, brother and sister, and then in later years my auntie lived with us too. Unfortunately, like many of us, I was brought up in a dysfunctional family environment, with domestic violence, parents struggling to make ends meet, and who didn't really seem to *like* each other, never mind *love* each other.

Maybe my parents did love each other for those first few years of married life, but I think they grew apart and disconnected enormously. They both had a lot of their own emotional pain to deal with prior to being married, and this, I believe, greatly affected their capacity to create a happy marriage and consequently prevented a happy family life.

Growing up, my memories of my father included his constant need to be working, and the times he was home he would absorb himself in watching TV and was exhausted. Even with the long hours that Dad worked, there always seemed to be financial struggle, so Mum went back to work part-time when we were all at school, so that there would be extra money for necessities.

It may have been a rare occurrence, however one that was so appreciated was when Mum would take my sister and I shopping at the local department store. It was a very happy memory, and I remember feeling much joy at being able to wear new clothes. I also felt lucky that Mum was a great housekeeper, a fabulous cook and prepared lovely meals for the family. Growing up, I always had a bed to sleep in, clothes to wear, and even though our clothes were minimal, mum always made sure they were well laundered and ironed.

I loved those days when I returned home from school and Mum had pressed all our clothes and placed them on our beds. Mum also loved to bake cakes and slices, and one of my favourites were her "fairy cakes" filled with fresh cream. How I loved my mum's baking. Sometimes it's sometimes the simple things that can bring us the greatest joys and bring us life-long happy memories.

I also vividly remember, as a child, that I was very scared, insecure and full of many fears, including the dark. My fear of the dark was so extreme I would even pretend to fall asleep on the sofa so I could delay having to go to bed to confront a dark room on my own. As I was the youngest, I was supposed to be the first to bed, so prior to going, mum would have to close the blinds before I would even enter the bedroom. I would also get her to check under the bed to make sure there were no monsters! I remember constantly feeling fearful and anxious throughout my whole childhood.

In 1970, I started primary school and, unfortunately, I had a very bad start. I remember my Prep teacher would smack the back of my knees with a ruler if I forgot my reader. This was a traumatic experience for a 5-year old, and thank goodness smacking in schools was eventually banned in the late 70's.

Luckily, the harsh discipline did not affect my reading or love for books; however, upon reflection, it definitely affected my self-worth. Our teachers can have a massive impact on our lives, for better or worse. There were many days I refused to go to school due to the fear of my teacher, and I would pretend I was sick so I could stay at home with Mum.

To make the situation worse, during my primary school years, I was bullied quite severely from my so-called friends. I remember being in

Grade 2 when I became friends with three new girls that had started in my class. I felt so happy to be a part of a group of girls, and at the time thought I was creating some lovely friendships.

It wasn't long before these friendships turned into a nightmare for me. They would take turns in bullying me, and I remember one lunchtime when they even put insects down my dress! These girls were supposed to be my friends, and yet they took delight in being so mean. The ridiculous thing was I would accept their apologies, and then I would think everything was okay again, and then the cycle would repeat.

Overall, my primary school years were mostly a horrible experience. I certainly did not have the courage to stand up for myself in those days. I felt I did not have a voice as a child, at school or at home, where I was the youngest. I was shut down many times, so did not feel I could voice my opinion. If I ever did speak up, I felt that I wasn't really heard. I would struggle with this for many years to come, and had to consciously work on having the courage to speak my truth.

One of the highlights of my childhood was I was extremely creative. I would write plays, create characters, and perform. Alongside my sister, we would create colourful characters, and we would take great pride in presenting and performing our plays. I felt like I was part of another world, a much nicer world to be in. When I was performing, I didn't feel any fear, only pure joy. It was also in these moments I felt I did have a "voice", and I could come out of my shyness when I was playing a part that wasn't myself.

I created various characters over the next few years, and on many occasions, I would always cast my sister as the "pretty girl" and I would cast myself as the "witch", or any kind of ugly character. When I was growing up, I really believed I was the ugly one. This was even emphasised by some family members, who referred to me as *the one with personality,* and to my sister as *the pretty one.*

There were many times throughout my childhood, teenage years, and even young adult-years, where I felt more comfortable with males. I found it difficult to make close female friends. I became a "tom boy" at around the age of 10, wearing Miller shirts and jeans and playing "British Bulldogs" in the school yard, mostly with the boys. I would climb trees and enjoyed playing marbles with them at lunchtime, as I found the girls far too nasty for my liking, and it was easier to avoid them. I remember feeling lonely, disconnected, and like I didn't truly fit in with any group.

Mum and Dad seemed to becoming even more disconnected from one another. I remember Mum sleeping on the couch for many months prior to them officially separating. I think Mum had a difficult time dealing with her unhappy marriage and previous traumas, so she did go through a stage where she drank quite a lot. Dad spent a lot of time out of the family home; however, when he was home, he was loving towards my sister and I and we loved him very much.

This was a different story with my brother, as he would get the strap when he didn't behave, and this occurred quite often (my brother had a very rebellious streak). The fear of getting the strap meant that my sister and I were extremely well behaved; we were both scared of being punished.

My sister and I actually feared my brother as he was so aggressive towards us both and was a horrible bully at times. Unfortunately, my sister and I didn't tell our parents as I think we just wanted to keep the peace and didn't want to hear another beating. In hindsight this was not a great way of dealing with our brother as he continued to get away with his bullying and aggressive behaviour throughout our whole child-hood. My sister told me that she knew from the age of 12 that she never wanted to be anything like my brother and that he was a horrid role-model as our eldest male sibling.

In 1976 there was a huge turning point in my life when Mum decided to finally separate from my father, after years of unhappiness. My nana had unfortunately just lost her second husband and was feeling enormous grief and loneliness, and offered her home to Mum, my auntie, my sister and myself. My brother stayed living with dad in our family home and it was lovely to live in all "girl" household.

I realise now that this would have been my mother's escape, as prior to that I think she felt trapped with nowhere else to go. Mum had little funds and little resources in those days, so she delayed leaving my father. There was no way my father was going to leave and give the house to mum and the children. I believe he even threatened mum with burning the house down, rather than giving her the family home. When my nana gave my mum a way out, she did not hesitate to leave.

The new journey began as my mother, sister, auntie, and I all moved in with my grandmother in the middle of 1976. I adored living with my grandmother, as she was a humble and loving woman. I also believe I inherited a lot of her intuitive abilities. She was a beautiful and compassionate woman.

The physical domestic abuse that occurred between my parents was always behind closed doors, and it was only in recent years that the extent of domestic abuse in our family home was revealed. After the separation, Mum would always protect Dad, as she didn't want to affect our relationship with him and so she never really talked to us about the abuse. There were always whisperings in Mum's family; however, I think Mum was also scared of Dad's "bad temper". She always wanted to keep the peace.

I started High School in 1977, and it became a much better world than those horrid primary school years. I developed some lovely new friendships, and overall my life seemed to improve. My sister and I spent every second weekend with our father, and our Mum seemed a lot happier. Life seemed more stable and it was like a whole new happier chapter was about to begin for me.

Your Path to Creating Creativity

Can you remember all those things you did as a child that made you squeal with happiness? Remember that feeling and that memory? If you can, then you will remember how great it felt. For all the dysfunctional things that we may have had to deal with as a child, most of us still experienced some fun, laughter and love.

As we progress on the path to adulthood, we often forget about what brings us the most joy. We get caught up in the stresses of life, the drudgery, our insecurities, and our fears. We forget that life doesn't really need to be overcomplicated to be happy. The thing is, once you are in JOY, you cannot feel pain.

We all need to make it a mission in life to always have components of joy in our lives. I recommend you create your **joy list** as this is a great reminder to make sure you are regularly bringing joy into your life. One of our missions should be to make sure we are as happy as possible, so we need to ensure we do what brings us joy. To be able to feel that deep sense of joy and peace in our hearts and souls daily will make us feel so much more alive, vibrant and help to create magnificence.

For all the laughter and fun you may have experienced as a child, did you still grow up with feelings such as:

- ❖ Not feeling good enough?
- ❖ Not feeling smart enough?
- ❖ Not feeling pretty enough?
- ❖ Disconnected, lonely, and feeling like a misfit?

If so, I can certainly relate to your pain, but it's time to move on from these feelings and to start a new journey of feeling good enough, feeling smart enough, and most definitely feeling love worthy. It's time for you to feel connected and feel a sense of belonging. One of the biggest challenges is our extreme lack of self-love and self-worth, but once we connect with improving on our own worth, life can change in amazing and miraculous ways.

Healing / Inner Child Work

Many of us continue to hold onto the pain and suffering of our pasts, which prevents us from living the best life possible in our present and our future. If you still feel wounded in any way from your childhood, I recommend you do some deep healing and inner-child work.

Find a therapist/healer that suits you, as you do not have to keep suffering. It's very probable your pain may be related to something from your childhood that you haven't yet cleared, and this inner-child pain may keep playing out, in one way or another, into your adulthood.

Tapping into Your Creativity

Tapping into my creativity certainly helped me to deal with my fears and insecurities as a young child, and it allowed me to escape from my pain. Personally, my creativity included: writing, acting, and producing plays. I also loved reading books, and I would completely escape into the world of fairy tales, especially with books written by Enid Blyton (my absolute favourite is "The Magic FarAway Tree"). **Remembering how I coped in childhood was a great reminder that returning to my joy is one of the biggest keys to finding my true purpose in life and increasing my happiness in so many ways.**

It's time for you to connect with your own creativity and ask yourself what you loved to do. Maybe you are still connected with your creativity, but like many of us, we get so caught up in our pain, we forget what brings us the most joy. If you have lost that connection to that creative part of you within, it's time to reconnect.

> *Connect to your passions – your JOY, your "sweet spots".*
> *Create your "joy list" or your "passion list" and refer*
> *to these lists regularly.*

Think about what inspired you and gave you joy. Improving your life may be as simple as going back to one of these things that you loved and you have forgotten about. Life can get in the way of our own passions, as we start mindlessly going through the motions of the day. We revert to "survival" mode rather than "thriving" mode.

When you are doing something you love to do, you will get that knowing feeling in your heart that it's something you are meant to be doing. You will also be in "creative flow" when you are utilising your gifts and you cannot help but feel more joy. I highly recommend you return to making time for the things that you love and the things that "light you up".

Recovering from Bullying

If you have ever had a close relationship with someone who has been bullied, or you have been bullied yourself, you will know we cannot underestimate the effects bullying can have on our lives. You can be bullied at varying ages, and under a multitude of different circumstances. Whether it be at school, at work, at home, in friendships, or in romantic relationships.

From my experience, there is no doubt that bullying can have a hugely negative impact on your life. I also believe until you clear this pain related to being bullied in the past, these issues may very well keep coming back, until you learn the lesson from being bullied, and heal from these experiences.

My low self-esteem and low sense of self-worth contributed to the reasons why I was bullied in the first place. The ways in which I put up with this type of behaviour, and attracted such horrid, nasty girls was a big red flag. I think people who are confident and have a higher self-worth do not usually attract bullying, particularly at school.

The childhood bullying scarred me for many years, and I think it prevented me from connecting to other girls and forming close friendships. There was certainly evidence of a huge disconnect, and at times I felt so lonely. I couldn't seem to find my "tribe" and didn't have many girlfriends that I trusted or felt totally comfortable with.

If you have been bullied, your self-esteem will have taken a beating, and you will need to implement a plan so you can rebuild it. You may also suffer from depression and feel weak, lack courage and feel helpless. It's also probable you don't want to tell anyone about what is happening, and you could be suffering in silence.

In my opinion, you should never ignore these symptoms, and you may need to open up and tell someone about what you are experiencing. I am afraid if you do not do this, your situation might very well get worse prior to it improving, as you are bottling everything up. This affects your confidence and sense of self, and it can also have a negative impact on your health.

I was bullied in the workplace only a few years ago, and I believe it happened because I didn't completely heal from the bullying of my past. **That's the thing about life lessons; until you learn the lesson, it will come back to "bite" you in some way**. It wasn't until I recognised that there was a link between my past and my present, and I realised I could then clear this pattern.

If you had low self-worth prior to being bullied, you may find it has worsened, and you will need to be proactive in your healing. You also need to know you are truly worthy of being treated with respect at all times. If you hold an energy around you that is projecting your insecurities, then how do you expect others to like or respect you? When you feel good about yourself and honour who you are as a person, no bullies or nasty people can affect you. Their words and actions would be like "water off a duck's back".

> *You need to know under no circumstances do you ever deserve to be bullied, discriminated against, or humiliated in any way.*

These are some of my key strategies in dealing with being bullied:
- o Reflect on your past, and if you realise you have suffered from bullying, get some therapy or healing to clear this old wound.
- o Build on your self-worth – invest in your own personal development.
- o If you are suffering from ongoing depression, which is highly likely if you are being bullied (or have been), please see a professional therapist to help you through this difficult time.
- o Learn to appreciate yourself and stop the self-negative talk.
- o Do things that make you feel better and bring you joy.
- o Journal your feelings and share them with someone who can help and support you.

Breaking your Parent's Cycle

Our parent's behaviour and pain can have a huge impact on our own behaviours. We often take on some of their behavioural patterns. This may include their negative conditioning, their lack of self-worth, and lack of self-love. Did you grow up with your own parents being abusive towards one another? If so, there could be a high probability that you allow yourself to attract abusive relationships. You may think it's normal to live a mediocre life, and you may feel stuck in your pain. You might not think you deserve complete happiness.

It has been a long and winding journey, to break the cycle of fears and insecurities that have been passed down by my parents and ancestors, and to realise my own life is valuable. You may also need to get to a point in your life where you know that you deserve a fabulous life, one in which you do not have to just settle for mediocrity. Remember, you are not destined to suffer.

Key Lessons:

- ❖ Be grateful for everything that you do have, instead of focusing on what you don't.
- ❖ Dream big, even when your situation and surroundings suggest otherwise.
- ❖ Break your parental and ancestral cycles of negativity. Recognise what brings you peace and joy – I call these your "sweet spots".
- ❖ Be open to healing/therapy to clear your suffering.
- ❖ Get support and speak to someone about your experiences of bullying.

For every child who has suffered trauma, insecurity, low self-esteem, no self-love, or very little self-worth, I dedicate this "LETTER" to you. If you are still suffering, realise you can overcome all the challenges from your past, and like me, you can become a strong warrior woman.

"A celebration of the woman that you have become"

Dear Beautiful Woman,

I know you have struggled, and you have experienced enormous trauma. I even know that as a little girl you were very insecure and you thought no one liked you. You had no confidence and very little self-love. You often felt alone and you were scared of everything. You felt like you never really fitted in. You would escape into a "make believe" world of fairy tales to dull the inner torment. You were often bullied at school, and you felt like you did not have a voice - no one really heard you. You felt ugly and worthless, and as a result, people often treated you badly.

Now, stand in front of the mirror and see that you are a wise, magnificent woman. You are a woman who is imperfectly perfect. You are strong and courageous, and you are not afraid to speak your truth. You have fought hard to become the woman you are today. You love and honour yourself deeply and are comfortable with who you are and what you stand for — you love your "inner-child" and you have become love worthy.

And how do I know all this? I am also that woman.

— Jo Worthy

"Always know that you are more than enough. You are precious, unique and worth being adored and treasured"

– Kandee Johnson

Lesson 2
You are Worthy Of Being Adored

A Truly Fated Meeting

In 1979 my whole life was going to change in ways that I could never have imagined. Allow me to take you back to when I was just 14 years old, and how it was at this very young age I began to fall madly in love with an amazing, loving and gorgeous young man (who was also very young - only 16 years at the time of this fated meeting).

Ironically, I met "John" at a "Parents Without Partners" Disco. My father took both my sister and I to this event one Saturday evening. That night, the DJ had a junior assistant in the form of this vibrant, lovely guy, who I was instantly attracted to.

"John" would become my first boyfriend, and the first guy I would fall deeply, madly in love with. After years of feeling anxious and unhappy, for the first time in my life I felt like one of the luckiest girls in the world. It was hard for me to even comprehend that I could feel so loved and adored.

I vividly remember going on our first date, and meeting him at the top of what used to be called Princess Park Station. I can clearly remember how much we kissed and cuddled, like two young lovebirds long separated and reunited once again. In those days, this particular railway station had a lovely rooftop garden with chairs to sit on, and it was reasonably private. Let's just say a lot of affection was exchanged, and I think it was in those moments I quickly learned the art of kissing. I also remember thinking he was a marvellous kisser with such lovely, sensual, full lips.

For our first date, the movie we selected was "The Life of Brian", and for the most part, we watched it and really enjoyed the movie. Even more so, we just loved being together from the very start. My first date has been imprinted on my memory, with remarkable clarity of detail. To this day, I wonder if he still remembers these times as vividly as I do.

We both knew from our first meeting, and then our first date, that we would become boyfriend and girlfriend. We had such a strong and immediate connection. Within a few months, it was like we had known each other forever, and we were connecting at a deep level. The attraction and the eventual love I felt for John was enormous, and difficult for many to fathom, as we were still so young.

I felt like I was walking on Cloud 9, and to be honest, I was amazed I could even get a boyfriend. At the time, I thought only the popular pretty girls and/or the ones with big bosoms got boyfriends. In those days, I certainly didn't feel very attractive. I thought I was too skinny, had very small breasts, and I also had to wear thick "bottle top" glasses due to being so near-sighted.

It dumbfounded me that he found me attractive and wanted to be my boyfriend. I felt ugly growing up as a young girl, was never very confident, and at times was extremely shy (unless I was in performance mode). I thought John was the best-looking guy in the whole universe, and I felt so blessed that he was such a beautiful person as well.

I only mention the small breasts part, as I was so self-conscious in those days and I longed for bigger breasts (be careful what you wish for, as they are a lot bigger these days!). The horrid boys at school would tease me for being "flat chested", and one boy at high school came up to me in my art class one day and grabbed me around my breasts and asked, "Where are your tits?" I was mortified and felt extremely humiliated! How could boys get away with such appalling behaviour at school?

My John ironically always reminded me of John Travolta, with those piercing green eyes, and he even had some of the moves — he loved to dance. He also had that eastern European sexiness about him, his father from Croatia and his mother was Serbian. We were like kindred spirits, reuniting with each other in this life. In fact, if it wasn't for the fact that we lived an hour apart and had to go to school, we would have been inseparable.

For young people with no licenses, it meant taking two separate trains to see each other. Although, believe me, I would have travelled a million miles to see this beautiful young man. At the time, he was the main person in my life who brought me happiness.

On weekends, we would take it in turns to visit each other. As we were both in high school, we only got to see each other on weekends and school holidays. To make things worse, we did not have mobile phones or social media as a means of communicating. I yearned for him during the week, and I remember thinking that Sunday nights to Thursday nights were impossibly long. The times we spent together were full of laughter and sharing our dreams. We were like best friends, only we were also very intimate and very affectionate toward one another.

I have always had a love of astrology and started studying it in my teens, so it's no surprise that I love to talk about the sun signs of my various boyfriends. John was a "Scorpio" sun sign, like me, and I found it interesting that I was at the very start of the sign and he was at the very end. Regardless, we shared lots of similarities and we were both very passionate, honest, loyal, and at times intense.

Other fond memories of John include how romantic he always was, making me home-made Valentine cards and writing poetry filled with so much adoration. I remember keeping those cards for many years as part of my sacred possessions. I will also never forget his lovely Serbian mother, making me crepes for breakfast on my weekend visits, and the fact that she loved having a girl in a male household. The fact that I was an Aussie girl going out with her precious boy was never an issue, and she always welcomed me with open arms and a huge heart.

I don't think you ever forget the power of that amazing first love. This relationship certainly taught me a lot about love, and it also taught me a lot about sex. On the weekends we could not get enough of each other and would always find ways to have sex— sometimes in some interesting places!

I feel blessed that my first sexual experience was so loving, as I believe this has a huge impact on our sexuality for our entire lives. I must say, sex was enjoyable; however, as you read my story, you will realise —at times— sex and intimacy wasn't always as healthy as my first experience.

We were like "Romeo and Juliet" – a young couple, both feeling deep love for each other. In fact, this beautiful young man wanted to marry me, but at the time I was too young to commit to marriage. So, instead of dealing with my fears of commitment after witnessing my parent's terrible marriage, what did I do? It was 1982 and just prior to my 18th birthday, I broke up with the most precious and amazing person in my life.

I broke his heart, but I also broke my own very fragile heart. As a consequence, I would suffer my first nervous breakdown within six months of my self-inflicted break-up with one of my great loves. This would be the beginning of my experience with ongoing mental health issues for the next four years.

As I sit here writing this on a beautiful, fragrant spring afternoon, I feel enormous warmth and care for this man. I realise in the span of a lifetime, our relationship lasted only a short while. My memories of my first love are cherished, and will reside in my heart forever. Thankyou dear John for allowing me to feel love and be loved – you will be in my heart for eternity.

Your Path to Creating Adoration

We all deserve to be adored, and I don't think there is a human being who doesn't want to be loved. Although, to be accepting of someone's adoration may be more of a challenge for some of us than others. I also believe we need to adore ourselves before we can fully embrace and accept being adored by another person.

Unfortunately, for many of us, we tend to learn the hard way. In my case, I completely rejected the love of a beautiful young man and sadly spent the next 25 years searching for that deep love once again. There are many reasons why we reject love, and of course **low self-worth** is the cornerstone to unhappiness. We can **self-sabotage** our own happiness, because we ultimately feel we are not deserving of it.

Increasing Self-Love

I suggest you consciously work on your self-love every day and know you are deserving of a loving and respectful relationship. You do not want to throw it away and suffer the awful consequences of rejecting the love of someone who is amazing, because of your own stupid fears.

I suppose the problem arises when you do not recognise the fears, and you do not understand at the time that you have no self-love. However, all the warning signs will be there, you just need to stop and think about your life and how you are living it. Be conscious and feel into your fear, journal it, and speak to someone you trust about how you are feeling.

> ***Do not reject love because of your own stupid fears – recognise your behaviour to prevent you from making an impetuous decision***

Even though I sought professional help at 18, I still wasn't fully conscious of my destructive behavioural patterns, and I would just go from relationship to relationship, searching for something I couldn't seem to find. **The answers were within me, not outside**. I was in fact totally disconnected from my inner-guidance and avoiding my true feelings, as it seemed to be an easier path to deal with.

Please look within to find your own answers and trust your intuition.

Please know you are worth so much more, and it **is essential for you to increase your awareness and work on yourself,** to stop being so impulsive and impetuous. Believe me, the consequences of rejecting love, (one that could have been the best experience of your life), will cause extreme suffering and torment within. Like me, you may spend years healing from the pain.

Self-Sabotage

I believe self-sabotage is one of the main reasons as to why we reject the adoration of others, even when we love them with all our heart and soul. **You have to ask yourself: is it your mindset of not feeling worthy enough that has stopped you from being loved and adored?** If you are feeling really unworthy, it's like you may as well just run and hide, rather than run the risk of actually being happy in your life.

When you reflect on some of your behaviours and decisions, do you think you have in the past, or are now self-sabotaging some of your own happiness? Have you witnessed your parent's unloving marriage and observed they were not great role models when it came to love and relationships? Have you unconsciously developed a fear of marriage? Of course, this is not an excuse to play the "blame game" with your parents; we need to be accountable for our own decisions, but these questions may assist you in the recognition of your own patterns and the reasons behind these patterns.

It can be difficult to understand self-sabotage at such a young age. In my case, looking back there was no doubt I loved this young man so very much, and yet I rejected him when he made it very clear he wanted to marry me. It's now easy to acknowledge my own fears and insecurities were coming into play. You need to make a firm decision **you are worth being loved and adored and stop the self-sabotage**.

Key Lessons when Dealing with Break-Ups:

Break-ups are horrible, and are a time in your life where you will need more support and assistance. Believe me, if I had a plan and extra support after my first break-up, my life would most likely have taken a very different path.

Let's face it, break-ups will happen to most of us. I have put together some key learnings and strategies for dealing with a break-up.

Get Professional Help / Healing

If you are experiencing a break-up, and you're finding it difficult to even get through the day; you are not sleeping, your behaviour is erratic, you cannot stop crying (even in public), and your nervous system is very strained, then you may find that seeking a therapist/healer could help you immensely with your healing and create more contentment in your life.

> *Be proactive with your mental health, tune into the warning signs that you need help so that you can take the necessary action*

It is essential that you take your health very seriously, and if you are depressed or suicidal please seek **urgent** professional help. Prevent yourself from resorting to negative patterns of behaviour, such as drugs, alcohol, sex, shopping, or food. This will only extend your recovery time, and may even set you up for some lifetime habits that are very difficult to break. When going through a break-up, be very gentle and nurturing to yourself, adopting even more self-care practices.

During a break-up, we experience many raw emotions, so adopting healthy practices to combat the effects of stress should be a lifestyle choice that is then ongoing. You will need extra fuel for your body with a focus on nutrition, especially during those first few weeks or months as your immune system will likely be weakened from the stress of the break-up.

Throughout this time, it could be very tempting to drink yourself stupid or take recreational drugs to avoid the pain, which could then lead to ongoing addictions. You should avoid these methods of escape under all circumstances, as your life could become a whole lot worse. At some point, we need to deal with loss and sorrow, otherwise, it can come back at a later stage and "bite you" when you least expect it. Numbing your pain with addictions will not allow you to move on and create a new and exciting life for yourself.

Treat Yourself Like Your Own Best Friend

During this difficult time, ask yourself: how would you treat a friend experiencing a break-up? I suggest you start treating yourself like this. **Be kind to yourself, be loving, and stop playing the blame game.** Stop the negative self-talk as well, every time you say something negative about yourself replace it with something positive. Believe me, it takes practice, but it will eventually become a habit.

Give yourself some slack, and stop over analysing what you could and should have done. It's okay to have a few days feeling sorry for yourself, but then you have to "get up, dress up and show up", as they say in the classics.

Self-Love Practices

Work on yourself and your self-love so that you can attract another amazing relationship. Though please do not settle for just anyone, simply because you might feel lonely and want some affection. Remember, a person alone is not going to fill that well of sorrow.

A life built on self-love is a very personal journey that you must continue. When you are in a state of vulnerability, you can quite often make some very extreme judgment calls, and potentially start a relationship with someone who is definitely not meant to bring you to your highest purpose.

During this difficult time, work on yourself as much as you possibly can, and put the focus totally on yourself. When you feel emotionally stronger, you may then begin to think about another committed relationship. Have fun and do not isolate yourself too much, or in contrast go to extremes of going out constantly. Find a lovely balance and really get to know you.

Move Your Body

Exercise more and move your body to release all that sorrow and stress. Dancing is another great way to release all the emotion. Even if it's turning up the music at home and dancing around the house. Yoga and meditation are also great for mind, body and soul. Swimming is highly recommended too, a great way to release some of that stored anger is to kick your legs like there is no tomorrow.

A punching bag may prove invaluable, especially if there has been betrayal within your previous relationship. I also suggest you go to a mountain and yell your lungs out, giving yourself permission to release tall that pent up anger from your body.

Journal Your Feelings

Keep a journal of how you are feeling and allow your emotions to flow; don't think too much about what you're writing – just aim to get all your thoughts out of your head. You can even burn the paper afterwards if you wish to, as this is also very cleansing. Spend time at home and if you need to, cry and howl like a baby, allowing all those emotions to be felt and flow out so they can be released.

Becoming Philosophical

Release all that negativity; in particular, stop thinking *"what is wrong with me?"* There is most likely nothing wrong with you, and you will need to accept that some relationships do not work out or are simply not meant to be long-term. Of course, there would have been faults on both sides, but understand the concept that some people come into your life for a "lesson, a blessing, or a lifetime".

I believe you can learn the most about yourself and about life during these really painful times of dealing with a break-up. Understand that it wasn't meant to be at this moment in your life, even if it seemed amazing, the universe has other plans for you, and there are most likely some deeper reasons why the relationship has ended.

Key Lessons:

- ❖ Heal from your last relationship prior to starting a new one.
- ❖ Take a step back from your busy life and heal from the loss, taking time for quiet reflection.
- ❖ Nurture and be very gentle on yourself.
- ❖ Work on your self-worth and do not settle for just any type of relationship, as it's better to be on your own than be in one that is not healthy.

> *"Pain or Pleasure? I say Pleasure"*
> — Epictetus

Lesson 3

You are Worthy of Pleasure

Sex, Dates & Rock n Roll

The next chapter of my life was filled with a lot of dating, sex, and listening to rock n roll. In my case, I would adopt many addictions throughout my life which would enable me to numb out my pain; however, luckily drug and alcohol addictions were not amongst them.

After I had split-up from one of the loves of my life, John, and before I could process my deepest feelings, I went straight back to the dating scene. I had a few months of just going out and meeting different guys, and many were just one-night stands. Even though I loved sex, and it was probably an adrenalin rush having sex with someone new, this type of behaviour was not very fulfilling for me. My heart was crying out for another big love, the kind of intensity and love that I had for my first boyfriend.

It's now clear to me this was another way I displayed addictive behaviour traits, and I was just using sex to dull my pain. In reality I still loved John, and instead of healing my wounds, I would just numb out my pain by having sex with guys that I hardly knew and didn't even connect with. Honouring my body and sexuality was going to take some time.

I was what was known as a "yes" girl, and it's a label that I now own completely. The sad thing was if I wasn't so private about my sex life, I would have definitely been "slut shamed". Unfortunately, many young girls were, and their behaviour most likely caused issues for them later on in life. Actually, growing up in the 70's and 80s, boys were often celebrated for having lots of sex with different partners; yet, girls would often be "slut shamed"!

The Racey song rings loudly in my ears "Some girls will, some girls wont', some girls need a lot of loving and some girls don't". Without a doubt, I was a young woman who needed a lot of "loving!" Although looking back, "loving" was not really loving in the true sense, and many times it was purely just loving in a very sexual primal way.

> *I didn't love me and men certainly didn't love me at this time in my life*

I didn't identify at the time that I was unconsciously being destructive. I just knew there was a certain unhappiness and void in my life, and I desperately wanted a "boyfriend" again. I didn't want a guy that I would just have sex with, and my behaviour was starting to make me feel empty inside. If I continued down this path of one-night stands and casual encounters, it would potentially become completely soul destroying for me. As much as I enjoyed sex, I appreciated that it had to have a deeper meaning for me.

My New European Family

For my 18th birthday, my sister and a few girlfriends ended up at a nightclub in St Kilda, called The Venue. This would be a very fated decision, as ironically, it was that night I was to meet my next boyfriend, who I'll call M#1 We would be together for the next two years.

M#1 and I both had a love for music, and songs by Van Morrison and Jimmy Hendrix were constantly playing on the tape deck (It was the 80's and we had tape decks in those days). I remember our "parking days", and those songs even to this day bring back memories of being with him. Music is definitely a powerful memory enhancer.

I certainly **never** pretended to be a "good girl", and I enjoyed sex with M#1, especially compared to a one-night stand, where there was mainly only a physical connection. At this time in my life, I can honestly say I never consciously felt any shame or guilt for being sexually active, or any notion that I had to be in love with a guy to have sex with him.

It didn't bother me that we had sex on the first night, because it felt right for me at the time. Many people would warn you that if you slept with a guy on the first night they wouldn't continue to date you and they would lose respect. This is clearly a generalisation, and you can be the only one to decide if this behaviour is right for you. In addition, if you have an instant connection, they are not going to lose any respect for you, this is just shaming BS!

I was really very fond of M#1, and he actually treated me very well. He was, admittedly, a little immature for his age, but he was loving, caring and funny. He could get aggressive with other people, and he also had some deep-rooted anger towards his own father that would play out from time to time.

During those two years together, I became a big part of their family and loved staying over, particularly on weekends. They were Croatian and his mother was a fabulous cook. To this day, I still use some of M#1 mother's recipes, and now appreciate her huge influence on my cooking style.

His mother adored me and we had a really close connection. I remember his mum hoping and wishing we would get married. In fact, M#1 did fall in love with me, and he wanted to marry me. Once again, my fear of marriage was triggered, and I really didn't want to get married at age 20. It's also true that this relationship was very different to my first boyfriend and my feelings were not as strong.

Even though I was very fond of M#1 and loved our time together over those two years, I don't think I ever fell madly in love with him. I was 20, and decided this was not the man I wanted to commit to any longer and had out-grown the relationship.

I knew I was still traumatised from my first relationship and longed to be with John. I still loved him and was actually continuing to emotionally torture myself for ending a relationship with a guy that I really deeply loved. It was devastating to me when I found out that he had well and truly moved on and, in actual fact, six months after I left him, he was with another girl and they were engaged. To say that this broke my heart was a huge understatement, and I didn't cope very well at all.

It was around this time in my life that I started to experience some mental episodes. I started seeing a psychiatrist, and I also began to make some very big decisions about my life. It was within a few months that I also resigned from my permanent full-time job. After a visit to Sydney for a weekend, I met a new guy, named A. I must have thought that I could "escape my emotional turmoil" so suddenly I decided on a whim to move to Sydney. My new adventure awaited and of course some very harsh life lessons would be experienced!

Your Path to Creating Pleasure

The path to creating more pleasure, especially sexual pleasure, can be wrought with frustration, outdated conditioning, and accompanied with strong feelings of guilt and shame. There are many ways in which we can incorporate pleasure into our lives, and sex is certainly high on many people's lists. However, we should not lose sight that we can derive pleasure in so many different ways. I would love for you to be able to feel vibrant and sexy in a range of ways, and to be able to live a fully pleasurable life.

Sex is Designed to be Pleasurable – Release the Shame

For many of us, sex might have entailed a combination of pleasure and pain. In my case, it has mostly been physically pleasurable, but, at times, has also been very emotionally painful. If you have been abused in any way, it can take a huge journey to eventually accept and celebrate pleasure, and there are often quite a few layers of healing to embark on before finding sexual pleasure and desire once again.

There should be no shame around enjoying sex, as it is designed to be pleasurable. For many years, women who were brought up in a religious environment, (which was common in previous generations), quite often related to sex as purely a means to procreate, and/or simply for making their husbands happy. But why would there be so many erogenous zones on our bodies if it were not meant to be pleasurable for us as well?

Luckily, we have come a long way from outdated beliefs and sexual shaming; however, for some of us born prior to the 70's, it can be a long journey to connect to more pleasure in our lives. This is particularly true if you were "slut shamed" when you were younger, if you were part of a very religious upbringing where it was customary to feel guilt or shame if you were sexually active prior to getting married, or if you have been sexually abused at some time in some way.

These factors can have a detrimental effect on many women, which can be unfortunately carried through into their mature years if they do not clear that energy from their past. Thank heavens our generation today does not have the same level of guilt associated with "sex prior to marriage", or having sex for pleasure. I am thankful that women are now more liberated, as the choice to become sexually active is a very personal choice, and should not be governed by what society thinks.

When it comes to your sexual practices, only you can decide what is right and wrong, but it should never be a dirty secret or a guilty pleasure.

Sex can be very pleasurable, and unless illegal, there should never be any guilt or shame attached to it. This will only lead to problems in the future and may even cause a dislike towards sex and/or an inability to derive any pleasure from sex.

In my opinion for any close relationship to be truly healthy it requires regular intimacy. Having sex and providing mutual pleasure is one of the most enjoyable ways that we can connect deeply with our partner. Being affectionate with one another, listening to one another, and supporting each other are great aphrodisiacs. It also is a great way to release day-to-day stresses and get back into our bodies.

It's Your Right to Enjoy Orgasms

Orgasmic pleasure will be a very personal journey for you, and I do suggest that if you have never had an orgasm, to do further exploration on yourself so you can experience this pleasure. Every woman deserves to experience this, and it's great to know how powerful our bodies are and how much stress we can release by love-making and self-pleasuring.

Healthy self-worth

Having a healthy view on sex can relate directly to how healthy your self-worth is. As young women, we need to realise if we have a healthy sense of self-worth, we will not usually want to share our bodies and have sex just for the sake of it. I also believe once you have a good dose of self-worth, you are far more likely to have clearer boundaries and, in turn, you will treat your body and your heart with much more respect.

If you are like me, you might have used sex to dull your pain. I hope you can see that this is self-abuse, and be aware you have further work to do to improve your self-worth so you can modify your behaviour. If I were single today, I have to admit I would prefer self-pleasure to sex with someone I didn't adore or feel any connection with. Personally, and from a lot of previous experience, sex is far more amazing with someone you are connected to, someone who will honour you and adore you.

Your Sex Life is No One Else's Business

Your sex-life and how you create pleasure is all about what feels right for you and how you understand what your personal values are. Sex is a very personal topic and you need to make the decisions as to what is right for you, where you are honouring yourself and your needs, without being destructive or self-abusive. It's no one else's business who, why, and when you have sex.

Trust Your Intuition

A great habit to adopt would be this: prior to becoming intimate with someone, connect with your inner-wisdom and ask if this is for your highest good. I know it can be difficult when we are swept up in the moment of passion; however, we often make some decisions that we would not have made, had we trusted our intuition in the first place.

I cannot change my past, and for that matter, neither can you. **What you can change is the present and your future.** You need to stop obsessing about all the "mistakes" you have made and wishing you had done things differently. You can learn to forgive yourself for allowing the second-rate relationship, for not allowing yourself to trust, for not using wise judgement and for not honouring your own beautiful body – your temple.

None of us are perfect, and many of us have made decisions that were not for our highest good. Believe me when I say that it's never too late to start trusting your intuition and asking for guidance. It's time for you to decide that from this point on, you will not accept anything in your life that does not serve you in the most positive of ways.

Releasing the Shame Around our Sexuality & Sensuality

It's time to release the "shame shit" if you feel shameful or guilty about your past behaviour, otherwise it will keep you imprisoned within your own self, limiting your ability to connect to your pleasure. You may even get to a point in your life where you think you have it all together, but underneath there is something that is not quite right.

You need to get rid of the "shame shit" as this can prevent you from truly connecting to sexual pleasure

Do you feel powerless at times? Do you also feel that a part of you is playing too small? Like me, you might also have to dig deeper with your healing, particularly if you have been abused. You may need to release any guilt about receiving and giving pleasure, as this will help you connect deeply to your pleasure zones when you do so. Sex is not a guilty secret and neither is self-pleasure. We all need to embrace our own "pleasure zones".

Connect with Your "Sexy Fiery Goddess"

I believe all women can be sexy. Whether you are single or in a relationship, it's time to connect with that "sexy fiery goddess". Sometimes she is buried deep inside, but she is still there and waiting for you to unify with her. You can even call on different goddesses to help you to embrace your sexiness and to ask for guidance to connect to your "sexy fiery goddess". Aphrodite is the perfect goddess to be able to do this.

Self-Care:

Looking after yourself and putting yourself first is a priority, and I believe this will also enable you to feel sexier. Get yourself a pedicure/manicure, moisturise your body — head to toe — and do it in a way that is sensual and has you connecting to your body. Have a bubble bath, aroma baths, massages, hair treatments, etc. The list could go on, but if you want to feel sexier, it's time to take care of you and adopt regular self-care practices. Do not wait for someone else to make you feel sexy.

Sexy Lingerie:

It's time to wear that sexy and sensual lingerie regularly, not just for special occasions, I believe it has a direct effect on how we feel as a woman. Whether I am wearing sexy lingerie just for me to see and feel it, or whether it's to add some spice to the bedroom, wearing sexy lingerie is highly recommended.

If you do have a partner, show off your physical assets, as it will make you feel sexy. When we feel sexy, we become sexier. Most lovers will really appreciate the effort you have put in, as well as being quite stimulated by the visually appealing lingerie. A little bit of role-play can also spice up the bedroom.

Life is too short to wear holey undies and saggy bras, so invest in some lacy or silky lingerie that feels gorgeous on your skin and makes you feel like a sexy and sensual goddess. Even if no one else can see your lingerie, you will have this mysterious sexiness about you because you'll be able to feel the sensual fabric rubbing against your soft skin.

Key Lessons:

- Love & honour yourself and make wiser decisions as to who to allow into your "inner sanctuary". Give your body to only those that deserve you.
- Base your decisions on your value system and not someone else's.
- Learn the art of self-pleasure, rather than relying on someone else to pleasure you; embracing self-pleasure and connecting to your "pleasure zones".
- Learn to recognise any negative behaviours, like utilising sex as a form of "numbing" yourself out.
- Know that you are deserving of real pleasure and there should be no guilt associated with this. Remove any "shame shit" when being sexually active and actually enjoy sex.
- Treat your body like a temple; with love and devotion. Admire what your body does for you and look after it as much as you can.

- ❖ Eliminate any feelings of not being sexy enough. It's a state of mind, so feel it, know it, and embrace that sexy part of yourself.
- ❖ Know that it is time to treat yourself like a goddess and invest in YOU with daily self-care practices, pampering days, attending luxurious retreats, day spas, and wearing sexy lingerie.

"Nourishing myself is a joyful experience, and I am worth the time spent on my healing"

– Louise Hay

Lesson 4

You Are Worthy of Healing

It was 1985, and I was 20 years of age, and probably felt a lot wiser than I actually was. Within a few months, I had decided to leave my two-year relationship, resign from my full-time job, leave my apartment that I was sharing with my sister, and leave Melbourne to start a new life in Sydney with a guy that I had just met. Some may say this was my fun adventurous spirit kicking in; however, beneath the surface it's clear to me now, I was just running away from my issues.

Impulsively, I had booked my bus ticket, packed my case, and I was off on my next adventure, leaving Melbourne on a Thursday night and arriving in Sydney on a Friday morning. Immediately, I started looking for a job and applied for a secretarial position that seemed suitable. As it turned out, they were interviewing on the weekend and by Sunday afternoon, they rang me and offered me the job! I accepted it, and by Monday morning I was starting a new job after being in Sydney for three days.

It was a relatively small company of engineers and architects with a "family like" environment. This was a huge blessing at the time, as I didn't have any real friends in Sydney, and only one relative. I stayed in that same job the entire 16 months I lived in Sydney, and ironically, this job was going to last longer than the relationship that I had moved there for in the first place.

Here I was, only 20 years of age, and following a weekend visit to Sydney where I had met this new guy, I had decided to move to a city that I really didn't even know. I had no job, not much money in the bank, and a naivety that (upon reflection) was scary.

Even though A seemed nice, he certainly didn't appear to be the most intelligent person I had ever met, and the conversations were never that stimulating. It's difficult to know what attracted me to him in the first place, except that he took an interest in me. Before I could even stop to reflect upon my life and deal with my issues, I was moving to Sydney and moving in with a guy that I hardly knew. This certainly would be one of many dumb decisions I would make throughout my life.

Some People are Just Not "Your People"

It wasn't long before I regretted my relationship choice. I found that the relationship itself was boring, and it also became evident that the feeling was mutual. He found me boring because I didn't smoke drugs, and because I loved to cook and bake cakes on the weekend. Basically, he was bored by me because I didn't like partying and I was actually a real home-body.

In fact, I was anti-drugs and I have never been a big drinker, and I remember A's "party" friends making fun of me and telling him I was a real "dag". They questioned what A saw in me. I had no connection with these people, but I nevertheless wondered why they couldn't accept me.

I was naive and I didn't realise then that we don't connect with every person that we meet. I was offended by their insults, and because of my lack of self-worth, I questioned my ways and thought my character was flawed. I would overly analyse, particularly when I didn't fit in, and I would wonder why certain people or groups didn't like me.

Luckily, with hindsight, I can identify that they were definitely not *my people*. We can't connect with everyone, and that's okay. We do not need to change to fit in with other people, and even in those days, I certainly wasn't going to smoke drugs or drink just to be accepted, no matter how low my self-worth was.

Falling Apart – Another Nervous Breakdown

Before I left this relationship with A, I started to become paranoid and experience some "episodes". My mind was beginning to struggle with what was real and what wasn't. I was taking two trains to work, and I found myself feeling so fearful, with the paranoia that everyone was talking about me.

At the time, I wasn't aware I was being completely delusional, and felt the whole world was conspiring against me. It was a huge indication of how unwell I actually was and I started to feel extreme fear and was even contemplating suicide. It got to the stage that I didn't trust myself with standing close to the platforms whilst waiting for trains, because I was starting to consider jumping in front of them.

Luckily, it was at this point I realised that I needed some serious help and took myself off to see a Doctor at a local clinic. When the Doctor discovered I was suicidal, and possibly psychotic, I received an appointment to see a psychiatrist immediately. The psychiatrist then admitted me into a private psychiatric clinic for urgent treatment, where I stayed for approximately two weeks.

I have vivid memories of this time in my life, and remember the medication we lined up for each night, consequently walking around in a "zombie" fashion as the medication caused so much drowsiness. I also became more creative, drawing, and writing in a journal, which was something I had not done for years.

When I got out of hospital, even though A had been supportive of me when I had my breakdown, we both knew the relationship was over. I found a place to live close to my job, and was once again officially single. Here I was, living in a city where I didn't have any friends, I no longer had a boyfriend, and I had just one relative that lived locally. My job was my only saving grace, and the fact that my work colleagues were so supportive of me. I returned to work without too much difficulty. I slowly but surely reduced my medication so I was able to work during normal office hours.

Please note I am not a Doctor and I am not suggesting anyone else should stop taking or reduce their medication unless they seek prior medical advice. This is purely representing my journey and mine alone.

Returning to My Home Town

After I recovered from my nervous breakdown, I decided to go back to Melbourne and initially lived with my Mum and Stepdad as I was settling back into life there. I was still healing from my breakdown initially however within a few months I started to feel strong enough to look for work once again.

Luckily, once I started applying for jobs, I was fortunate enough to get another position very quickly. Once the job was confirmed, I was able to start looking for a flat-mate, who ended up being one of my sister's contacts. I felt very grateful, as I had my own place to live and was able to secure a job that was local to my new abode.

My life seemed to be getting back into a nice even flow, and I was feeling very pleased with what I was now creating. I moved back to my home town, which was enjoyable for me, as I could see Mum, Dad and my sister more frequently and attend family functions. I had a good job working as a personal assistant in the computing industry. I really enjoyed this job as I felt an integral part of the team and was developing some great skills, including being introduced to the Apple Mac world, and organising people/events.

I loved my new job and stayed with the company for over two years, which was an exceptionally good record for me. The only reason I left this particular job was under unique circumstances, where my boss had left and my role didn't really exist any longer, as they were closing down that part of the division.

While at this company I engaged in a brief office affair, even though it was usually a no-no for me to get involved with a work colleague. This affair was very light and fun with no real expectations of settling down with each other. We were basically "friends with benefits".

During the course of our fun together, I remember spending one Christmas Day in bed. We were both eating chocolates and drinking champagne and enjoying other sensual delights. I find it quite amusing to reflect on this memory, as I had obviously boycotted our family Christmas that year (that part is quite fuzzy!). This was evidence that the new Jo was emerging and I could "dance to the beat of my own drum". I felt a great sense of freedom and peace, and was feeling like my life was finally in flow and that I didn't have the need to conform to other people's expectations.

Your Path to Healing

Your personal path to healing can be a long journey, but I think it's a path we must continue if we want to live the best possible life. Without healing from our past suffering, we will continue to lead a mediocre life.

One of the keys to healing is to firstly acknowledge what needs to be healed. Once you become more conscious of your issues, you can then get the help you require, and start a plan that will assist you on the journey.

You cannot run away from your problems

I certainly encountered some huge lessons along the way, and a big one was even though you go and live in another place, you will still take your "baggage" with you. **Your problems do not miraculously disappear because of your change in environment – they actually go with you wherever you go.**

Have you moved to a different suburb, state, or even country thinking that all your problems will be solved because of the relocation? When we adopt this approach we are running away from our issues, and we're not being conscious about our lives.

If you are currently in a situation where you want to move away because your life is so unhappy, take a step back and genuinely think about whether changing your location is going to really change anything. In some cases, it might, but for most of us, we are just running away and ignoring the real issues.

Please don't make the same mistake as me, and think that things will automatically change just because you have changed your environment. I also recommend not to make big life changes when mental health is compromised, as good judgment and clarity is lacking in these tough moments.

When you are dealing with mental illness and extremely low self-worth, you can inadvertently make very bad decisions that are not for your highest good. **Settling for a bad or incompatible relationship is a big warning sign that you need to improve your self-worth.** If you learn anything from my story, it's that you should not settle for the second or third option.

We cannot run away from our issues and we need to deal with them head-on. I realise that it takes a lot of courage, but I could have saved myself a lot less grief, if I had sought the help I needed, and not been so ridiculously impulsive.

Start Investing in Yourself

Personal development books could help improve your life and help you to become a better version of you. Reading can not only be inspirational, but can also increase your awareness, knowledge, and help you to make the necessary changes to improve your life. There are so many courses, workshops, and events that we can attend to increase our knowledge and become inspired.

The Power of our Minds

One of the books that still continues to have a huge impact on helping me improve my mindset and change some very negative thought patterns that were ingrained in me, is "The Power of the Spoken Mind" by Florence Scovel-Shinn.

Florence's books opened up a whole new world to me, and I started to understand that we are the master of our lives, and we can control our thoughts and actions. I knew I had a lot of work to do and was aware I had been conditioned to communicate and think in a negative way. As a child, I had moments of "thinking and dreaming big"; but was held back by this inherent negative self-talk that seemed to be insidious.

After reading this powerful book it started me on a new journey that continues today. I learned to utilise the fundamentals of the law of attraction, including the power of the mind to visualise the exact life that I wanted to live. In conjunction with positive affirmations, I was really starting to change my life and direction with a much more positive mindset.

I started testing this theory and began visualising the exact life I wanted to create. This enabled me to start creating clarity in my life instead of just "winging it" or, alternatively, making rash decisions. I had become the master of not thinking about my life in any detail, and was finally starting to distinguish between what I wanted and what I did not want.

Visualisations and affirmations became a regular habit of mine, and I actually started to experience some successes. Every day I visualised I was mentally well, and my health certainly improved in all areas. Of course, I was combining these practices with some practical healthy habits as well.

Bringing Joy Back into Your Life

I adored reading as a young girl, so it was great to become an avid reader once more, and was extremely happy that at long last one of my passions had returned. Sometimes we look for complicated solutions to improve our lives, when often the answer is far less complicated.

Mind/Body Connection & Self-Love Practices

Another pivotal book I read in 1985/86, was Louise Hay's, now legendary *"You Can Heal Your Life"*. Louise's work is very well known now and has proven to be life-changing, not only for myself, but for millions of others around the world. It should be noted, however, that Louise's book took many years to become a best-seller, as people were not as open-minded about their healing or her theories in the 80's. It wasn't until the 90's that people really started to look outside the box for alternative ways of healing. Now, luckily for us, natural healing and being more open-minded with various remedies has become a way of life. I love that many people now look to alternative ways, as well as traditional methods, to heal themselves.

I still continue to be influenced by Louise's work to this day, and highly recommend her philosophies and powerful mindset practices. Also, the mirror work that she teaches is so powerful and highly recommended to increase your self-love and your overall wellbeing.

The mirror work consists of concentrating and looking into your eyes, into a mirror and telling yourself that you love you, you appreciate and honour you, and there is no judgement on self.

This practice is not about fixing up your hair and/or make-up, it's simply connecting to your soul via your eyes. Like anything new, its uncomfortable at first, but then it's something you become accustomed to. For me, I now actually love this practice and feel proud of my strength, wisdom and courage and I witness this as I look deeply into my own eyes.

The mind and body connection to ailments is also fascinating, and I have personally found it to be very accurate. Every disease in our body, I believe, is attached to an unresolved emotion in our body. In Louise's famous bestseller, there is an alphabetical listing on various ailments and what they mean emotionally, and also great affirmations that you can reference to coincide with your particular disease. It's amazing work that I continue to use for myself, and would highly recommend it to my family, friends, and clients.

Bless these authors, as their work made an enormous impact on my life and I am very grateful to them for having the courage to publish their books. Through the trauma, pain, and moments of extreme darkness, I managed to see some light, thanks to their work. I really recommend you search for your own "teachers" and find books that are transformational and inspiring to you.

So back in Melbourne, I was feeling extremely content with my life and I was really making a huge effort to work on myself. My goal was to become more insightful and more conscious. My affirmations and visualisations became a daily habit, and I also had my passion back for reading again, especially anything that had to do with personal development and self-improvement.

I continued to eat healthy food, I didn't go out and party, I didn't do drugs and I limited my alcohol consumption. I was really starting to really feel a lot more balanced. It was at this time in my life I discovered that I didn't have to be a victim for the rest of my life, and I was responsible for my own happiness – it was no one else's responsibility. Maybe I was finally growing up and becoming accountable! I knew I still had a lot of work to do on myself, and there were still many fears and insecurities to tackle, but I knew I was making progress.

On reflection, visualising what I wanted to create and practicing daily affirmations to increase my health and abundance, was a catalyst to improving my life. I really noticed that my life was starting to change, and one of the biggest changes was that I stopped having mental health issues, and my confidence and outlook was far more positive.

Affirmations

I have had some amazing changes occur when I have used affirmations. I applied a lot of the material that I was reading, and even though at times I massively lost my way, when reverting back to some of the fundamentals of the Law of Attraction, my life would "miraculously" improve.. Once you create your own affirmations you can type them up, have them around your house, and read them as often as you can.

Even if at first you are uncomfortable and do not believe what you are saying, know that your mind is very powerful. So, if you continue to feed it with positive messages, eventually the belief will become a habit and you will start to see improvements in your life.

Key Lessons:

- Becoming real about your life and realise where you need to improve.
- Invest in yourself – reading, researching, personal development.
- Make your own personal list noting all the things that you love to do (For me at this time it was reading, theatre, astrology.)
- Utilise the power of affirmations.
- Utilise the power of visualisations.
- Early nights – getting at least 8-9 hours sleep per night.
- Nourishing your body with wise food choices.
- Very little or no alcohol.
- Regular exercise – get your body moving.

"Daring to Set Boundaries Is About Having the Courage to Love Ourselves even when we risk disappointing others"

– Brené Brown

Lesson 5

You are Worthy of Creating Boundaries

From 1986 – 1990, I dated a variety of men and, unfortunately some of them, it turned out were already married. I refer to them as the "unavailable man". I wasn't consciously going out to find an "unavailable man", however, they seemed to be attracted to me and I was actively pursued by them. There were many times where I didn't even discover that they were married, until well into dating them. Deception would unfortunately become a pattern in my life.

My theory is that energetically, I was attracting the "unavailable man", because of my own fears and insecurities. It was a very unhealthy pattern. Subconsciously, I was attracting these types of relationships because of my own lack of self-worth and huge fear of commitment.

I did actually get to meet some great men who were highly intelligent, and we would often share interesting conversations about life, travel adventures and human behaviour. I think at some level I did realise that these types of relationships were never going to be serious, and I think it was also a way to avoid anything deeper. If I had been more balanced, or possessed a healthier sense of pride and self-worth, I would never have got involved with them in the first place, or continued my involvement after I found out they were actually committed to someone else.

It was now 1990, and I was 25 years of age. I had not had a serious relationship since I was 20. My flatmate was going on a road trip to

Adelaide, and asked me if I wanted to join him. It sounded like fun and as I had never visited Adelaide before, I happily agreed.

On the final night in Adelaide, I wanted to go to the Casino as I had never been to one in my life and was curious. My flatmate wanted an early night, so I decided I would experience a solo adventure. I got myself all glammed up, wearing my favourite black velvet mini dress, high heels, and I even wore my sexy red lacy underwear. This decision to go out that night was going to be another massive turning point in my life.

When I arrived at the Casino, I felt uncomfortable in the new and unfamiliar environment. I clearly remember the moment when I saw a roulette wheel. I felt mesmerised by the game; however, I didn't really understand how it all worked. I went to buy a drink, and then proceeded to take the escalator downstairs, and as I was heading down, I was a bit taken aback by a tall, handsome man waiting at the end. He appeared to be looking straight at me with a big, beaming smile. I took a glance over my shoulder, to make sure it was me he was looking at, rather than someone else behind me. I then saw that I was the only one on the escalator.

As I reached the bottom, this very friendly man boldly asked me my name and if I would like to have a drink with him. Again, I was a bit surprised; however, his smile, charm and friendly nature was very appealing. I agreed to go and have a drink with T. I was single after all and felt flattered by the attention.

My fascination with Astrology led me to ask him very early in the evening when T's birthday was, and it was no surprise to me that he was a Leo Sun sign, as he quickly displayed some typical characteristics of this sign. In true typical "Leo" lavish style, T ordered a very expensive bottle of champagne for us to share.

I could not believe how easily we connected. Our conversation seemed effortless. I had at least three glasses of the delightful champagne, which was a lot for me, and I remember feeling a little drunk and giddy. The giddiness was emphasised by the excitement and the suspense of the passion that what was about to follow. Let's just say, I was relieved that I had actually worn the sexy red lace lingerie, even though I did not consciously predict having a night of passion.

Meeting my new lover, T in Adelaide was quite ironic, considering we both lived in Melbourne, and we even found that we frequented some of the same places in our home town. However, that lovely "bubble" was about to burst on our return flight to Melbourne, when T decided to explain that his life was presently "complicated". I'm sure I would have given him one of those looks, and wondered what on earth was going to come out of this man's mouth. I had heard the "complicated" word before, and my heart sank.

These feelings were substantiated as T confessed that he was, in fact, actually married. OMFG – NO not another one! Underneath, I was thinking, sarcastically, "thanks for telling me from the start of our encounter", although I knew from experience that it's common for some men to leave this very important detail out of the equation when you first meet. He went on to explain that he really wanted the marriage to be over, and T begged me to be patient, as he sincerely wanted an ongoing relationship with me.

Breaking the Cycle of the Unavailable Man

At this stage in my life, I truthfully had enough of being involved with the "unavailable man", and I told my new lover when we returned to Melbourne that I was thankful for the lovely few days in Adelaide, however, I could not and would not be part of a love triangle. I was adamant that T needed to go and work on his marriage and do everything possible to save it.

Thank goodness I was finally starting to set some boundaries in my life and I was no longer going to accept a relationship with an "unavailable man". The problem was I still was not firm enough with him, as he continued to ring me at work, even when I asked him to stop.

I was not responsible for him constantly calling me, and sometimes T would even arrive at my doorstep, begging me to take him back! I just kept telling him to go back to his wife and work it out, and to leave me alone. Finally, he did, and while I admit it was hard, it was something that had to be done, as I did not want a relationship with someone who was committed to another woman.

It's wise to not always judge the "other woman", because we often try and end or stop contact with the "unavailable man", who is actively pursuing, ringing, visiting and continuing to communicate, even when we ask them not to. We are not married or committed to anyone else, we are not lying or being deceitful, yet we will often be the one who has to take the backlash for being a mean woman who breaks up marriages!

After a few months of being single once again, and feeling heartbroken, I met a lovely older man, K, who to my relief, was also **single**. We started dating and I quickly realised that K was an extremely intelligent, passionate and caring man. The problem was that a huge part of me was missing my "Adelaide lover" T, and K was no fool and he easily sensed my detachment and lack of commitment.

I remember thinking K is such a genuine and loving person, why can't I just be content with him? To be honest, it was probably only the second time in my life I was with someone who was not only passionate, caring and intelligent, but extremely adventurous as well. This was rare and had only happened once before with John and I had also rejected his love.

Now that I am a lot wiser, my question would be "was my self-love still so low that I couldn't even accept love and adoration from amazing guys?" Why did I have to search out the "bad boys" or the ones that were unhinged, deceitful and unavailable?

This was a distinct pattern that I would eventually realise that I would have to change if I was to live a "magnificent" life. Unfortunately at this time in my life, I wasn't as wise or evolved and this pattern would haunt me as I continue to attract so many toxic and even abusive men.

K was very intuitive, and he knew a part of me longed to be with my "Adelaide lover", T. He was physically unable to have children and had spent a lot of his years fostering children with his ex-wife. K saw me as this 25-year old woman that would most likely want kids eventually, and he knew he would not be able to provide that.

Eventually, the "Adelaide lover", T actually did leave his wife, and K found out from mutual friends that this had happened. K was the one to tell me and encouraged me to contact T. In his mind, he thought I would probably be happier with my T, so he sacrificed our relationship and he never fought to save it. After dating for a few months, I did end up falling in love with my T and we started planning our new life together. We found a beautifully renovated apartment and one that was very close to the beach and the shops/cafes.

I thought T was extremely entertaining, funny and very charismatic, with a huge, generous heart. We never argued and we seemed to connect so effortlessly. Living together also seemed quite natural, and it was like we were meant to be. I can honestly say at this time in my life I was blissfully happy.

I was falling more in love each day, and I was feeling very healthy and fit. I really felt that my life was now in control, and was truly blessed. I couldn't wait to find out what adventures would come my way with my new-found happiness and fabulous life that was finally in front of me. Maybe I was starting to become Love Worthy?

Your Path to Creating Boundaries

You may have also struggled throughout your life to create solid healthy boundaries, and you may have also been attracting the "unavailable man", due to your low self-worth and struggle with the whole concept of self-love. Is your childhood conditioning ringing loudly in your ears, telling you that it is selfish to love yourself?

My conditioning was deep, and it would prove to be a huge journey to start to fall in love with myself. My self-love journey would eventually allow me to set clearer boundaries. It was certainly an area that I needed to work on and make some profound changes.

Perhaps you too have developed a fear of commitment due to some unresolved trauma related to your previous relationships. If you feel that the "unavailable man" has become a theme in your life, you might benefit from some deeper healing and reflection so you can stop this toxic cycle.

Also, and more importantly, understand **you are worth more than a mediocre relationship**. If you are going to put yourself and your heart on the line and sacrifice your time and energy, make sure it's for someone who will be worth it and for someone that can also commit to you.

> *Don't ever be someone else's second option and know that you deserve so much more!*

Setting Boundaries - Miracles

Once you start setting clear boundaries, your life will begin to change in miraculous ways. You need to take a stand right now and start treating yourself like you would treat your own best friend. DO NOT put up with anyone treating you badly, or accept yourself as someone's second option. Be realistic, because if someone is already committed in a relationship, you are their second option.

Once you have set clear boundaries as to what you will and will not accept in your world, you will notice people starting to treat you with more respect. **People only get away with treating you badly if you allow this to happen**. If you do not respect and honour yourself, how do you expect others to?

You need to make a conscious effort to change your behaviour and what you will and won't tolerate, so you can change the types of people you attract into your life and raise your vibration.

Invest in Your Personal Development

Invest in your personal development. This will be one of the best investments that you will ever make. If you recognise that you have a trait that could be improved on, read, research and take classes to work on your behaviour and increase your knowledge.

If you start off implementing small changes, and continue to add other changes, you will then continue to gain strength the more you practice these new behaviours. It may seem difficult at first, like anything new; however, it will become a valuable habit; and one that will serve you for years to come.

For example, if you are shy and feel you don't have the courage to stand up for yourself to voice your opinion, I recommend you seek help in becoming more assertive.

For me, I recognised I needed some assistance with becoming more assertive, so I bought books on this subject to help me. I read them vigorously and implemented some of the key strategies. With dedication, focus and resilience, I believe you can change any negative behavioural habit.

It became blatantly clear that I had **not** been creating very strong boundaries in my life. I had made myself available to anyone who accepted me, even when I was not compatible, or I knew there was no meaning or love in the relationship. **I constantly lacked clarity and direction and did not discriminate about who I got involved with,** thus putting up with **terrible mediocre relationships.** When I started to consciously think about my life, there were clearly some big themes that I identified. These "themes" included often taking the "second option" as I didn't value myself enough to say no to relationships that were not suitable. I was attracting a lot of dysfunction in my life, which caused deep feelings of constant unhappiness and despair. I knew I had to change if I wanted my life to change for the better.

Accept the Good and Reject the Bad

It is now easy to look back on my **inability to stabilise any form of relationship,** as I would either reject the good ones or take too long to leave the toxic ones. **I craved love, I craved stability and my actions were in complete contrast to my desires**. I jumped from relationship to relationship, and hoped that I would find some form of happiness and peace.

Your life often gets worse before it gets better, and this happened with my relationships. That is, until you learn your lessons. Some of the relationships I formed were extremely abusive, and I shudder when I think how I let it happen to me. I attracted toxic relationships, which was an indication of how low my self-worth was.

It would be wise for you to think about your own life in terms of relationships that you have attracted, and recognise some of the negative behaviour patterns you may have adopted. Have you learned your own lessons, or do they keep repeating themselves? Stop, reflect, and think about how you can move forward and create much healthier and loving relationships. Know that deep down in your heart and soul this is what you deserve.

When you love and honour yourself, you will be able to set healthier boundaries, enabling you to attract much more amazing relationships

When you love and respect yourself, this will be one of the biggest keys to increasing joy, peace and love in your life. It is absolutely essential to work on your self-love, if you truly want to live the life of your dreams. Once you have developed a love for yourself with healthy boundaries, you can attract the right partner and you will **not** accept the mediocre, non-committed, half-baked relationships.

You get what you think you deserve, so be very careful about what you think you deserve.

Becoming Accountable

I think that becoming accountable for your own life, and NOT playing the blame game, is one of the ways we can heal from the past and create a much more fabulous life. To be able to own everything that has happened to you is extremely refreshing and allows you to move past your suffering.

One of my common statements throughout this book is that **we cannot change our pasts, but we sure can change our present and our future**. Another phrase I love and often repeat is **the past does not define our future.** What's done is done, and you need to acknowledge this fact, and implement new strategies, so the same mistakes are not made over and over again. Stop hanging onto pain that is not serving you. **Don't ever live with regrets, as this will stop you from being magnificent and will block your abundance and flow.**

Having low self-worth and little self-love is a dangerous game leading to terrible decisions, unless you wake up and do the work to improve your mindset and your own worth. **The most important** thing in life is to consciously improve your self-worth and self-love, so that you can truly step into your power and start to live a magnificent life.

It's time to stop the following:

- ❖ Negative self-talk – ban it completely.
- ❖ Disrespecting YOU. How can expect others to respect you if you don't respect yourself?
- ❖ Attracting toxic and/or abusive relationships.
- ❖ Making rash decisions and creating instability.

Key Lessons:

- ❖ Don't settle for the second, third or fourth option.
- ❖ Don't allow yourself to be someone else's second, third or fourth option.
- ❖ Know your worth and stop allowing others to take advantage of you.
- ❖ Value 'YOU' and what you stand for.
- ❖ Back yourself every time – be loyal to 'YOU'.
- ❖ Set strong healthy boundaries that align with your value system.
- ❖ Give yourself permission to say that you are done with toxic people and situations.
- ❖ Improve your mindset, continue with required healing and continue to commit to your personal development as this will be your most cherished investment.

"Opulence is the law of the universe, an abundant supply for every need if nothing is put in the way of its coming"

– Ralph Waldo Trine

Lesson 6

You are Worthy of Opulence

After growing up with parents who struggled financially, and being known as the family who lived in the worst house in our street, I always had this burning desire to live in gorgeous homes. I certainly did not want to be classified as poor and struggle financially for the rest of my life, and I could still envision my life improving.

I often felt out of place in my family, as I would sometimes verbalise my visualisations and some of my family members would criticise me for being a "big dreamer" and roll their eyes. Some would torment and laugh at me, implying that my dreams were impossible.

Believe or not, as cliché as it sounds, I also had a vision of meeting a tall, dark handsome man who was ambitious, and that we would create a life together that would be very opulent. I envisioned a big, beautiful Federation style white house, with large sash windows and high ceilings, complete with a pool and beautifully landscaped English and French inspired gardens.

I also think that reading all those fairy tales as a young girl obviously had a huge effect on me as to what my expectations were. Even though I hate to admit it, I was probably looking for my "knight in shining armour" to save me. If only I knew back then that **I was the only one who could "save me", not another person,** I could have prevented a lot of pain.

It seemed like I may have finally found my "Knight", and T and I continued to live in our inner-city bayside apartment until we decided we would buy a house together. T's parents had a beach house on the Mornington Peninsula and T loved that area and he was certainly familiar with it. In addition, because we had limited funds and only a small deposit at the time, a house further out from the city was within our budget. The rationale was that it was a wiser financial decision to get back into the property market, rather than paying high rent.

I loved our life in our beachside inner-city pad, and even though it seemed like a good financial decision, I was very reluctant to move down to the Mornington Peninsula full time. Not only did I love and adore the vibe of living inner city and the lifestyle that it provided, it was also extremely convenient to commute to my work at the time.

Because I was in love with T and he was very insistent that I move with him, I found it very difficult **not** to (I was still suffering the "people-pleasers" syndrome). After little consideration, I made the decision to permanently move into our home, rather than it be a weekend escape.

Unfortunately, I had to commute to the city for work and this took over two hours each way, including driving part of the way and then getting dropped off at the train station. This was not really sustainable and the travelling was certainly taking its toll on my energy levels. After a few months of commuting, ironically, I was offered a redundancy package and decided to accept. This actually turned out to be a great decision, as it was only a few weeks after actually leaving my job, I found out that I was pregnant with our daughter!

Motherhood

This was a very exciting time of my life and I (mostly) loved being pregnant. I was 27 years of age, and I was now in a very committed relationship. Combined with my redundancy package, T was earning an excellent income through the family business, and we had just bought our first home together as a couple. Everything seemed like divine timing, especially as I was also expecting our first baby.

At this stage of our relationship, we both had been contemplating marriage, and with the pending birth of our first daughter, I was uncertain as to whether I would wait for our baby to be born before getting married, or get married before the birth. I kept changing my mind, and then all of a sudden, I decided at eight months pregnant we should get married so I organised an intimate but lavish wedding ceremony and luncheon at very short notice.

T and I were both very blessed to announce the birth of our beautiful daughter, who was born in January of 1993. The birth was tough and at times, the pain was intense afterwards. I found motherhood difficult to adjust to in those first few months. There were sleepless nights as our daughter was awake every 3-4 hours, and it was difficult to adjust to the sleep deprivation and the constant flow of nappy changing.

Being a new mother was a whole new world for me to explore, and there were no instruction manuals given to new parents! I felt enormously lonely, and it was the first time in my life I had not worked in a "job", which created even more feelings of isolation. But I was fortunate, as I did not have to work to pay the bills, and I could choose to be a full-time mother without the financial stress.

I would take our daughter out most days, if it wasn't shopping for groceries, or catching up with a friend, it was going down to one of the beautiful beaches. "Mother's Beach" became one of my favourites, and my daughter and I would spend many a summer's morning there. I also felt very blessed as I would frequently shop for beautiful collector pieces and homewares for our home; clothes and toys for our daughter, and a collection of gorgeous dresses purchased from some lovely boutiques in the area.

I slowly became more comfortable with being a mother, and I joined a mother's group and made some new local friends. I was fortunate to get on very well with my in-laws and for those first few years, we spent a lot of time at either one of their family homes. My mother-in-law was becoming very close to her newest granddaughter, and would lavish her with gifts, and was very loving towards her. We had quite a few family Christmases spent either at their beach house or their suburban home, and we were also very lucky to also enjoy family holidays at their apartment on the Gold Coast (my 2nd home!).

At this time in my life, I did feel very blessed and extremely lucky for everyone and everything in my life. My husband was exceptionally generous to me and was forever surprising me with lovely extravagant gifts. I vividly remember being in a local boutique whilst on holidays on the Gold Coast, and trying on some clothes in the changing rooms. My husband had disappeared for a while and then all of a sudden, he came back with a gold diamond bracelet which he threw over the change room and said "Here you go darling – this may match your dress", or something to that effect.

I had taken charge of the financials, including bill paying, and even though we lived a very opulent and delicious lifestyle with the income that was earned, we were still able to save quite a lot every week. We both had dreams of buying a more lavish home in the very near future, and our dreams were aligned with the type of home that we both wanted to buy and live in.

When our daughter was six months old we purchased a much nicer home in a more prestigious area. This house was substantially bigger, offering four bedrooms, two bathrooms, formal dining, lounge and large open family room, complete with a fabulous backyard for entertaining, and lovely landscaped gardens.

It still wasn't our "dream home", but it was definitely an upgrade to our first home. We continued to make plans towards the goal of buying our Federation style "dream home", which would come complete with an in-ground pool, big stately rooms, high ceilings and all the modern conveniences while maintaining period features. My vision of this dream home was still firmly imprinted in my mind and I never doubted that we could achieve this dream.

It was also at this time that I found an amazing cleaner/babysitter, who attended our home for a weekly clean, and in addition provide other services such as ironing and babysitting. This wonderful lady, Olivia became part of my family and I even took both her and her husband away with us on one of our numerous trips, so my husband and I could enjoy nights out together. They became like my surrogate parents, and I loved them dearly, as I would my own family.

I am constantly reminded of this house when I see photos of our daughter, in particular when looking back at photos of her 1st birthday party. We enjoyed many family celebrations in this house for the approximately 18 months we were there, and I certainly have many fond memories. It was after this time that we decided to buy an even more lavish home, and in actual fact, this would be our absolute dream home – the big white Federation style home that I had envisioned, with the gorgeous garden.

I felt well and truly blessed to be living such an opulent lifestyle, and at this time in my life I thought my childhood dreams had come true. I chose to stay at home and enjoyed the freedom of being a full-time mum, not having the stress of working long hours each day and battling with traffic and child-care arrangements.

I also had a husband whom I loved and adored, and the most beautiful baby girl. I also loved having my step-daughter over every 2nd weekend and had built a lovely relationship with her and enjoyed her company. I was extremely grateful for the life that we had created and felt that everything I had dreamed about had come true.

Your Path to Opulence

The term "opulence" means different things to different people, but regardless of your meaning I still believe an opulent lifestyle is available to each and every one of us. Whatever your definition of opulence is, I want to ask you:

Do you think you are worthy of opulence?

As soon as you answer this question, notice - what comes up for you? If the answer is no, then there is further work that you may need to do on actually believing your worth. You need to feel it and believe it and then go and create it. I also feel that creating opulence is related to believing that you are worth it.

As mentioned, your interpretation of "opulence" is most likely very different to mine. However, my belief is that everyone has the right to lead a life where you live in a beautiful home, travel to great destinations and wear clothes and shoes that not only make you feel great, but that make the most of your physical assets.

Childhood Conditioning – Your Belief System

You need to believe that opulence is your birthright just as much as anyone else's. If you are wanting to create an opulent lifestyle; and you are finding that you are not successful with it, you may first need to clear the conditioning of your childhood. For example, some of my family members would often laugh at me because I had dreams of living an opulent lifestyle.

Break the patterns and expectations of your parents and stop repeating their mistakes. We all have the power to change even the most extreme childhood conditioning.

I had a reasonably clear vision of what I wanted for my future. Though looking back, I could have been far more specific with what I wanted, to prevent attracting what I ultimately did. Admittedly I did attract regular employment, a first husband who provided a lush lifestyle, and I did get the beautiful house that I imagined, and the beautiful dresses and shoes.

The thing with affirmations and visualisations is that the more specific you are, the more the universe is aware of exactly what you want to create, and can help you. Remember when applying these powerful concepts, **you also need to be as detailed as possible and really think about what you are wishing for.**

> *Be careful what you wish for and be as detailed and specific as possible when you are applying visualisations and affirmations*

This was part of the formula I really needed to improve on. Had I also included that I wanted to attract honesty, integrity, and a loving and respectful relationship first and foremost, my life would have probably been very different. You are deserving of a beautiful home, clothing and travel, paying bills and savings; however, do not leave out the things that matter the most.

Don't Lose Sight of Your Dreams

Never lose sight of your dreams and visions, and continue on your path, no matter what barriers you have to contend with or what breakthroughs you need to experience. There will be, no doubt, times in your life where you will come across the naysayers. You will need to build your resilience, so you can keep your dreams alive, so they become a reality.

Do not be deterred when others laugh at you. Instead, stand strong with your convictions and to other people's differing opinions. I know that this can be tough if your self-worth is low, that's why it's so crucial to work on increasing your worth. Hopefully you can get to a point in your life where you have increased your worth and you are confident that you do not have to agree with everyone. It's far more interesting to have your own opinions and be courageous enough to express them, even if you are in the minority.

A Beautiful Home

After living in quite a few prestigious homes over the years, I know now that it doesn't necessarily have to be a big mansion, but it must be a home that is full of love, peace and beauty. We can create beauty wherever we live, whether that be a studio apartment, through to a mansion, or anything in between. The most important thing is that you are proud of the place where you reside and you have made it a "home". This is my new version of "opulence".

As a child, I felt ashamed of our house, and was bullied and humiliated because we lived in the worst house in the street. Dad was a hoarder and there was often rubbish or plumbing supplies out the front, and the façade looked a little shabby and run down. It would have been very easy to limit my thoughts and consider that this was the type of home I expected to have in the future. However, I had other ideas and I was determined **not** to repeat this pattern. I knew from a young age that I would not continue to live in a house that I was embarrassed of, but one that was beautiful, and I was proud of.

Some people define "rich" as having a roof over your head, food in your belly and surrounded by loved ones. This is the bare minimum we all deserve, but I also believe we can all create a more "opulent" lifestyle than just the basics of food, clothing and shelter. There is absolutely nothing wrong with dreaming big. Actually, I recommend it.

> *When you change your mindset, you can achieve so much more than you ever expected*

I have witnessed many people caught up in a "victim mentality" and not feeling worthy of opulence. They become jealous and resentful of what others have or deemed to have. They are not happy for the success of others, as they compare, whine about their lives and then they make statements like "Oh it's all right for them". They stay in this mode of being toxic, and then they wonder why they lead a mediocre life. They might even question as to why they cannot lead an opulent life.

Wearing Beautiful Clothes/Shoes

As a child, I longed to wear beautiful clothes, and felt ashamed of wearing shoes that had holes in them. I was bullied at school because of my clothing and felt humiliated. I understand that wearing beautiful clothes may not seem important to some; however, in my view, part of having a high self-worth and self-respect is taking pride in your appearance, and for me I want to wear the best clothes that I can.

You may not necessarily want to wear designer labels — that's a personal decision, however, make the most of what you have and wear the best clothes you can afford that look great on you. You don't have to spend a lot of money to look great. I highly recommend a fashion stylist to assist you in this area – there are so many wonderful stylists available to choose from.

Be Confident, and Shine Brightly

I have met many women who have focussed so much on their inner-work that they forget to embrace all parts of themselves. It is not pretentious or superficial to want to look good and make the most of what you have. Dress to suit your figure and wear clothes that are flattering, and always choose colours that make you feel and look good. It *does* make a difference and you deserve to be the best version of you.

Stop judging other women who are well groomed and polished who obviously put a lot of thought into their appearance. Like many of us, they may well have been to hell and back to become the woman that they are now. They have most likely connected to their own version of "opulence", invested in themselves, changed their mindset, and know that they are their biggest investment.

Compliment them, honour them and take a "leaf from their book" on how you may be able to do the same. **Celebrate other women and feel inspired and motivated by others rather than comparing and feeling jealous, as this will only hinder your own development.**

Travelling the World

As I have matured, I have grown to understand that it's not just about accumulating "stuff", but enriching our lives and spending money on experiences for our development, which is more important than anything. Travelling is a great way to spend your money, as memories are priceless.

I want to ask you- what are your travel plans? Where do you want to go that will excite you? Uplift you? Restore and relax you? You can take holidays that have different themes, some may be adventurous and full of sightseeing, and others may involve lazing around the pool or beach, reading, writing and complete relaxation.

Your life is precious and life is for living. Travelling will make your life more amazing and you will definitely feel more opulent as you travel around the world, becoming 'rich' on life experiences.

Key Lessons:

- ❖ Know that you are worthy & deserving of opulence.
- ❖ Reflect on your childhood conditioning and your belief systems.

- ❖ Utilise Affirmations / Visualisations / Action / Belief Principles.
- ❖ Stop the judgments, jealousies and critical behaviour towards others, as this will block your own "opulence".
- ❖ Recognise your "victim mentality", and make a conscious choice to change it and know that you are worth an opulent and amazing life as much as anyone else.
- ❖ Add fun and adventure to your life, spending your money on travelling, experiences, and creating wonderful memories.
- ❖ Spend more money on your personal development.
- ❖ Dream big and keep your vision alive.
- ❖ Be resilient and stop comparing yourself to others.

"The truth is rarely pure and never simple"

– Oscar Wilde

Lesson 7

You are Worthy of Truth

Despite our opulence my life didn't get any better and, in actual fact, it became my own living nightmare. It was approximately early 1995 and I was about to receive one of the biggest shocks of my life, where everything was about to change for the worse. Actually, my life was about to go to complete shit!

It was one night after dinner that the doorbell rang unexpectedly. When I answered the door, I was shocked to find two detectives standing there asking to speak with my husband. I excused myself from those initial discussions as I was getting our daughter ready for bed.

I remember my husband telling me that his daughter (my step-daughter whom I loved), had been to the school counsellor and had reported that he had sexually abused her. His beautiful daughter at this time was 15, and the detectives reported that she had been abused by her natural father (my husband!) since the age of 11!

I can recall being in complete shock and thought that I was actually hearing things. Was this some sort of very bad, sick joke? From the very beginning of these accusations, my husband flatly denied any claims of abusing his daughter from his 2nd marriage and very convincingly said she was making up the whole story. His reasoning at the time was that she was jealous that we had started a new life together.

As his wife, I thought I knew him so very well, and it didn't seem at all possible that these allegations could be correct, so I stupidly and naively believed him. How could my husband, that man that I loved, be a child sex offender? To make it even worse, how could he have done this to his own daughter? This was completely incomprehensible to me, and the mere thought of it being true was very sickening.

There were absolutely no indications to me that there had been any indecent or inappropriate behaviour happening under our roof, although it would soon be revealed just how deceitful and opportunistic he really was.Unfortunately, it was a period of time where I would be confronted with a lot of lies. There were even accusations that claimed these horrible actions took place in our marital bed when I wasn't home. I remember my husband had some very heated discussions with his ex-wife, as he continued to deny all of the accusations.

This was a time in my life where I felt like the universe had just given me a big whack across the face. I naively thought that I had an amazing life, and I was so grateful being married to a man whom I deeply loved, trusted and adored, and together brought a beautiful baby into this world. How could the man that I slept with every night, the father of my child, even be capable of this? It was beyond comprehension to think that he could be accused of such atrocities.

I would have thought that a child sex offender would be perverted in such a way that it would be more obvious. With regard to our own sex life I thought that it was fairly healthy, meaning it was regular and was nothing bizarre or abnormal. This was a very naïve perspective!

Prior to these accusations, this was a time in our lives where everything was just coming together beautifully, and I thought we were blissfully happy. Unfortunately, I was blissfully ignorant. I had been so excited that we had purchased our "dream" home and the exact house that I had envisioned had been manifested! What I did not envisage, however, was marrying a child sex offender!

We had only been in our "dream" home for a few weeks and I remember waking up one morning after we had settled into our glorious new home, and there was my husband, sitting at the family room table, head down, hands over his face sobbing uncontrollably. I asked T what was wrong as I sat down beside him. It was fortunate that I was sitting down, for what I was about to hear was going to crush every dream and every feeling about my husband.

T answered, looking me in the eye and saying: "**I confess and I want you to know that the allegations that I have denied are actually all true**". I distinctly remember looking at him and being in absolute disbelief. It was as though what T was saying and confessing to, was not what I was hearing, or more to the point, wanted to hear.

T instantly pleaded with me saying he was so sorry and then used the excuse that he was grieving for his first daughter from his 1st marriage (who had died at the age of 17 of a drug overdose). I remember T saying something like "I don't know what got into me" and "I don't know how I could do this to my own daughter".

At that time, I did not know the extent of the abuse, which would be revealed later in court. While T was confessing, a huge part of what he was saying wasn't really sinking in. I think I was in absolute shock and I didn't want to believe his confession, so the easiest way to cope was to just numb out my feelings and go into denial and be the dutiful "wife".

I did not want to face the very painful truth of what my husband had done and who he truly was. My old pattern of numbing out my pain had returned in the most horrific of circumstances. My life became what I could only describe as a very bad dream, and I remember I just wanted to wake up and hope and pray that it wasn't true! This was my way of coping with the trauma and magnitude of this terrible confession.

I woke up every day trying to put on a show that everything was really okay, and burying my feelings so I did not have to confront them. I didn't want to fall apart or lose control as I had my daughter who needed my love and support. Consciously or sub-consciously, who would want to admit that the man they loved and adored was a child sex offender?

I was supporting my husband through the court case, and it's difficult to put into words how I was coping with the enormity of what he had done. I remember describing it as being in a complete daze and not fully comprehending his actions. At this point, I still loved my husband, even though what he had done was completely sickening, as I didn't believe or want to believe the truth even after his confession. I just wanted my life back, my so called adoring loving husband – not this beyond comprehension occurences that I was confronted with.

It was only a matter of time, before I would eventually have to face even more dramatic truths and my marriage would then be on a very short life-span. It would become blatantly obvious that I could never trust T around our daughter, and how could I even think about being intimate with T ever again? The person that I thought I loved was actually not existent – he was like a figment of my imagination. I had been fooled and I felt very foolish. This was NOT the man I fell in love with, and this was not the father that I wanted for my daughter.

It was fairly clear from our legal team that T would get time in prison, it was just a matter of how long it would be. I decided it was better to sell our "dream" home, as I didn't want the extra stress of paying a mortgage while T was in prison. Even though his parents promised to continue to pay me a wage from their company so we could keep the house and pay the mortgage, I decided I didn't want that reliance on my in-laws (this would prove to be a wise decision).

After we sold the "dream" home, and prior to my husband going to jail, we settled on a cottage that we bought outright. This cottage was a humble property and required a lot of renovations and I remember very clearly walking into my new property and crying in shock and disbelief when it hit me that I was no longer living in my "dream" home. Luckily, I had good vision and the refurbishment would be a great project that I could preoccupy myself with, which prevented me from thinking about what the consequences would be when my husband went to jail.

Never be Complacent

Upon reflection, our "dream" home was in fact the nightmare house, with such short but horrid memories of my husband confessing to being a child sex offender. Some people can appear to have it all, including the handsome husband, the child, the beautiful home and what appears to be a normal, happy, and opulent life. My life couldn't have been further from the truth, except for still having my beautiful daughter, there were so many lies, betrayals and sick revelations to deal with.

I had certainly come down to earth with a big thud and this was a harsh lesson in complacency. It was at this time I really had no choice, but to decide that I had to be strong and rebuild my life, not just for my sake, but for my daughter's sake. To be honest, I wasn't really sure how I was going to do that, as my dream life had been shattered, and merely thinking about the future was too damn scary.

Your Path to Truth

It's imperative that we live a life of truth. Being truthful with ourselves and expecting the truth from our loved ones is "not negotiable". When you commit to someone, at the very least, you have an expectation that they will be truthful.

To be deceived is a horrid feeling and can be soul destroying. We all need to believe we are worthy of being told the truth. We also need to be fully truthful with our lives and what we are attracting. This can be very confrontational when you have attracted some horrible people and events into your world.

My relationship with T was full of dishonesty. I did learn that when you are dealing with a sexual predator, they are exceptionally good at deceiving you. However, there are also many other types of people where deceiving is just a part of their natural tendency. Unfortunately, I was going to experience this as well.

For me I had to question why I would even attract a man like this, one that had so many dark hidden secrets. I still don't exactly know why, but the only thing that I can put it down to is that **my self-worth was still very low and I was attracting lower level vibrational energy into my life**. I was not protecting my energy and was very careless, by allowing people of such low vibrational energy to enter my inner sanctuary.

Work on increasing your own worth and utilise daily self-love practices.

Protect your energy

ALWAYS protect your energy, particularly if you are empathic and very sensitive to other people's energies. Many people who have dark energy will be attracted to your light. You also need to be able to raise your own vibration so you are not attracting lower vibrations.

Protect yourself by visualising a beautiful big dome around your AURA, and do this EVERYDAY. Use crystals to help with protection, in your home, your office, and take some with you even when travelling.

Unfortunately, there are some very negative and toxic people in the world, and you will need to protect yourself from these lower energies. Do not allow your aura to be so open. Do not be naive to think that you are okay and you won't attract this type of energy. This was another harsh lesson for me as I was like an open vessel.

> *Don't allow yourself to be an open vessel – Protect your energy to prevent lower vibrations being attracted to you*

Honesty is the Best Policy

When you are in a committed relationship, you expect your partner to be honest with you. You also believe that you know your partner and you would think that there are no deep dark secrets that could be revealed.

My story may be extreme, and I don't suppose too many of you reading my book would have married a child sex offender; however, you may have experienced disgraceful lies in some other form. For me personally, lying is probably one of the worst things. Anyone who is an honest person will know how horrible it feels to be lied to.

Many liars, of course, believe their own lies. They are very convincing and most think they will never be found out and it's their natural disposition to be dishonest. People that lie have a pattern, and it's similar to the old saying that a "leopard does not change its spots". This means that if you have been lied to by someone, they are mostly likely repeat offenders, and may very well continue to lie.

In a healthy relationship, this is not something that I consider you should ever tolerate. If you are continually lied to and you accept it, it is really an indication that you have low self-worth and that you need to create some healthier boundaries.

You need to realise that you deserve the absolute truth, even if that truth is often very painful.

Many times, the clues will be there but we tend to ignore them. In the case of my first husband, there actually were no clues, but in other relationships where there has been dishonesty, when I really think about it, there definitely were clues.

When you are in a new relationship and you are getting to know this unfamiliar person, take note and be aware of any strange contradictory behaviour. They say that a good liar also needs to have a great memory as well. They often slip-up and contradict themselves.

Stay consciously aware as much as you possibly can, particularly when you are still getting to know someone. As much as we would love to, we cannot always trust everything we're told. It's often actions that speak louder than words. Be observant, take note, and don't think you are being silly by questioning certain contradictory behaviour.

Break Your Pattern and Stop Attracting Liars

You do not want to waste your time with someone who is not honest. Being with a dishonest person will only create a lot of pain for you in the long run. **Remember, you deserve better. Stop allowing people to lie to you**. Break the pattern if you find that you are constantly attracting liars and cheats.

If there is something within you that is attracting this, then you will need to dig a bit deeper so you can clear this pattern. You do not have to put up with anyone telling you lies. This is another example of attracting a lower vibrational energy.

> *Deception is nasty so decide right now NOT to allow it in your life ever again.*

You need to have enough self-worth to not tolerate people in your life that are dishonest. These chronic liars are being delusional as they are not really as they seem and their "mask" is not revealing who they really are. There are so many levels of lying; start to become a little more discriminating and aware of any contradictions and odd behaviour.

Liar Liar Pants on Fire

I was amazed to find that throughout my life, I encountered people who think that lying is completely acceptable. On many occasions, I believe liars will continue to deny that they have even lied. In my experience, I find serial liars are not evolved human beings, and will **not** take responsibility for their dishonesty, preferring to white-wash their behaviour. They may even go to the extent of saying that you're crazy, and what you heard was wrong, and that you are confused. This is such typical behaviour and known as gas-lighting, which is where you are manipulated to the point that they deliberately want you to question your own sanity. In addition, playing the blame game is very easy for them.

Repeat offenders should be avoided at all costs, as they quite often have lived their whole lives as liars, and it is their natural instinct to not be honest. Some people "couldn't lie straight in bed" as they say, and of course, remember the funny saying that we often hear, "Liar Liar Pants on Fire". These are very common phrases and very fitting for people that are liars.

Diplomacy Combined with Honesty

Honesty is the best policy, but it is also the way you say things, not just what you say. Many people think they have to be dishonest, as they lack the courage to be truthful. In most of these circumstances, these are predominantly referred to as "white lies".

Telling a "white lie" is clearly not something as serious, and people will often do this to prevent someone getting hurt or to protect them. These are not the type of lies and dishonesty that are a huge problem, although I do not recommend even a "white lie", as they could set up a pattern of lying about things more substantial.

I personally prefer to be honest in all circumstances, and that can be tough sometimes, because you don't want to hurt someone unnecessarily, or maybe you are living in fear and scared of telling the truth. In most circumstances, diplomacy is the best approach and allows us to be honest without being too harsh. At times, truths do hurt, but if we can be as loving and as diplomatic as possible, it is always better to be truthful.

Being Honest with Yourself

Honesty is also about being completely honest with yourself. It starts with you, and you need to stop lying to yourself. I constantly put myself down and questioned my own self-worth for many years, with lies like I am not good enough, or pretty enough, or smart enough.

Also, do not take on what others may have said about you, especially if it was in the heat of the moment. They may have called you names that were not very flattering out of anger. Please try to not accept any insults, even though this can be difficult if you have been verbally abused and you're upset and emotional. Please remember that **you are not what someone else has said about you, and you can eventually rise above their verbal abuse.**

It's also time to get real about your life and start to be conscious of your behaviours, patterns, and habits. Some of your habits may need to be changed, and once you get really honest with yourself, that's when you can start making the necessary changes.

Key Lessons:

- ❖ Be truthful about who you are attracting into your life.
- ❖ Work on your worth if you have created toxic patterns.
- ❖ Raise your own vibration so you are not attracting lower vibrations.
- ❖ Protect your energy – do not be an open vessel.
- ❖ Be aware of repeat offenders – they do not change unless they have deep ongoing therapy.
- ❖ Create healthier boundaries and do not accept lying.
- ❖ The truth is often painful but it can set you free.
- ❖ Be alert for dishonest behaviour patterns when you meet someone and you are still getting to know them.
- ❖ Actions speak louder than words.
- ❖ Don't waste your time with serial liars – you deserve so much better.
- ❖ Be the change you want to see – always be honest and have integrity.
- ❖ Be honest with yourself and stop telling yourself lies about YOU

"When a deep injury is done to us, we never heal until we forgive"

– Nelson Mandela

Lesson 8

You are Worthy of Forgiveness

When I first met my first husband T, he did seem a little eccentric but he appeared relatively "normal". He came across as happy, self-motivated and was exceptionally likable. In fact, T's behaviour did not appear to be abnormal to me in any way. Although during the course of our dating, and in particular when we moved into together, I could not work out why we were going through so much food.

I loved buying beautiful fresh produce and going to the markets, then returning home to prepare delicious meals. It seemed odd that there were never any left-overs, and entire contents of the fridge would often be cleaned out by the morning. There were some tell-tale signs that something wasn't quite right as T was always obsessed with his weight, constantly weighing himself in every house he lived in, he would install a sauna and use it daily.

I was approximately six months pregnant, and after a lot of questioning from me, was when T actually revealed to me that he had bulimia. Finally, it all made sense as to why we had no food left in the fridge in the morning. It was also why T was such a night owl as these "practices" were carried out at night when I had gone to bed to avoid detection.

Once T admitted that he had bulimia, I saw this as a "call for help". I began the task of researching psychiatrists and I found an excellent one who specialised in eating disorders. My husband wasn't that keen on the idea at first; however, I insisted that he needed to do this not only for his own sake and health and wellbeing, but for the sake of our relationship and our child.

The Court Case

It was during T's court case that seeing a psychiatrist was going to work in his favour, as the courts looked more favourably on perpetrators that sought help for their sickness. Ironically, T had initially started seeing the Doctor purely for his eating disorder, not for his urges to sexually abuse children. I discovered that T had this eating disorder for over 20 years, and bulimia had become a very bad habit and a pattern well and truly ingrained in his daily practices.

After two days in court, in November 1995 my husband would be convicted for Indecent Assault and Perverting the Course of Justice. The extra charge of Perverting the Course of Justice was because he had tried to buy his way out of his situation when he offered his ex-wife money if she dropped the charges.

The QC lawyer who we were receiving advice from at the time, suggested that "rich daddy buy ex-wife out". This was terrible legal advice especially from such a senior lawyer, and because of the extra charge, my husband would receive a three-year sentence to serve a minimum of 18 months, if he was well behaved and did all the therapy that sex offenders were required to undertake whilst in prison.

There are parts of the court case I remember clearly, while others parts are a blur. On the first day, I do recall briefly meeting my husband's first wife (there were multiple wives – I was his fourth!) and the mother of his first daughter, who had sadly died of a drug overdose at the age of 17. Her death had happened prior to me meeting my husband, so unfortunately, I had never met her.

It was the second day of the court case where another HUGE revelation would unfold, which I would not become aware of until after my husband went to prison. His first wife went to the media and what she reported would completely change my course of action and wake me up from my numbness.

The first wife was at the court purely for one purpose: she wanted to see T be accountable for what he had done to their daughter. She reported to the media that T had also interfered with their first daughter and that is why this daughter had become a drug addict and was now dead due to an overdose!

It was sickening to think that my husband had even used the excuse of grieving for his first daughter as a reason for offending his second daughter. I didn't think it was possible to be more shocked than I was before, but this was even more distressing. T had used the first daughter's death as an excuse but apparently, T had abused his first daughter when she was 18 months old!

Maybe I needed one more shock to comprehend exactly what sort of man I was dealing with. It was at this point when I knew that I was married to a complete sexual predator who had ruined his first daughter's life, and could potentially ruin his second daughter's life with what he had done. I also wondered with horror if he had done anything of the kind with our own daughter.

I could only imagine the pain of what his ex-wives were going through, as the mere thought of my own daughter being a victim to child abuse was beyond comprehension. This was all way too much to grasp, although it made me see that there were no more delusions of my marriage surviving.

Grieving – My Husband had Already "Died" in My Eyes.

Initially when my husband first when to jail, I just felt sad and I missed him so much. I do remember feeling like he had died and that the grief on some days was very overwhelming. In a sense, he had died in my eyes, as he was not the husband that I thought I had married – far from it!

I don't think you ever really come to terms with something as serious and as heartbreaking. The best thing that you can learn to do is to forgive yourself for allowing yourself to attract a man that was so deranged in the first place. Going through an experience as extreme as this, leaves you profoundly changed in many ways. You learn to navigate your life very differently, and your innocence and trust for others can be deeply damaged. That is, until you get the healing that is required, and forgiveness becomes a huge factor in your journey.

My life had completely spiralled to absolute shit in a matter of a few months. How could things change so dramatically in such a short time? This was a very **harsh and extreme lesson on truth**! I had to go home that night of the final day in court and face the fact that I no longer had a husband and I no longer had a "real" father to my child. It's only a very sick individual that sexually abuses any child, never mind their own flesh and blood! My life and my daughter's life would never again be the same.

I felt extremely lonely when I was living in my house with just my three-year old daughter, without a husband whom I would normally spend every day with. The man who I thought was my best friend, and whom **my entire life revolved around**. He was now going to become a fading memory, and so was my relationship with his parents and his sister who I had become very fond of.

To the outside world, I probably appeared "normal" and in control; however, a part of me felt like something inside had died. I wondered if I could ever get back to some form of "normality", if my heart could ever be healed, and if it would ever be possible to feel love again. Could I ever forgive my husband and could I forgive his family for turning their back on their grand-daughter?

I knew that I had to so that both my daughter and I could lead a more peaceful life?

More importantly, could I forgive myself for attracting someone like this in the first place? Instead of thinking "what the fuck has just happened to my fairy tale life", **I just numbed out any emotions** and started living a very sad and mediocre life for quite a while.

When I knew that I was definitely going to get a divorce, the in-laws (who had promised to support me) completely cut me off financially and emotionally. In fact, they refused to have any contact with me, which meant also avoiding their beautiful granddaughter. I was fortunate that my intuition had paid off regarding the downsizing of our house, so at least I wouldn't have to pay a large mortgage every week.

The family that I had become so close to, behaved like they did not even exist in our world. My mother-in-law had made one attempt to give her granddaughter Christmas presents, but when I initially refused to see her because of was so upset that she knew that her son had child sexual tendencies, that was the last I heard from her for many years to come.

Who could blame me for being so angry with her? Especially if these new allegations were correct and she was potentially aware that her son had interfered with his first daughter. I think once I confronted her and I was so fraught with anger, the guilt kept her away, as I believe she didn't want to face the very harsh truths that her son was in fact a child sex offender and now a repeat offender!

My resentment towards my mother-in-law was intense for quite a few years (until I could release and forgive) as T's first wife would swear that she knew that her son had these tendencies and didn't want to admit it or even deal with it in any way. That's why it's so sad as he offended one again to my vulnerable step-daughter years later and the fact that he could have been inappropriate to our daughter was beyond painful.

For me, it was easier to start living a mediocre life and be in denial, than be honest with what had happened and how I was really feeling underneath the protective layers and the "mask". Unfortunately, I was going to start living very destructively, attracting other horrible and abusive relationships and gambling my heart out to prevent the real truth. I think my state of mind at the time was in chaos and complete "survival" mode and my life was going to get a whole lot worse than I ever thought was possible.

Your Path to Forgiveness

Learning to forgive yourself for allowing horrible situations to occur and allowing toxic and abusive people into your life, is imperative if we want to live a magnificent life. It's also a relief to know that it's not necessarily about forgiving the other person, it's about forgiving YOU for allowing this to happen in the first place.

For example, I do not need to forgive my sex offender 1st husband, as I believe what he did is unforgivable, although I do think he was a very damaged soul who needed a lot of healing and probably will in his next lifetime as well. More importantly, I needed to forgive myself for attracting this calibre of person and for being fooled. The person that I fell in love with was a completely different person to the child sex offender that was eventually revealed to me.

There was a lot of forgiveness required on my part. I also had to forgive myself for having a daughter with him – a person that could never be a true father. I also hoped that my daughter could forgive me for choosing him, and understand that she was part of us both, because of my choice in partners.

This is an extreme example of forgiveness; however, it's a very real and raw example for me. Your story of forgiveness will be unique, but regardless, forgiveness can be challenging and it may be something that happens over a long period of time.

There are quite often so many different layers to deal with and there may be times when you need to dig deep to release any suffering and ultimately forgive yourself. Sometimes it's far easier to forgive another than ourselves, but we need to be able to do this, otherwise it's just another level of unwanted "energy" that remains in our bodies and prevents us from living our best life.

In my case, to say that I needed to dig deep and find it within me to forgive was HUGE, considering what I had just contended with in my life. However, even though a part of me was very destructive with my unconscious behaviour, especially the gambling and attracting low-life vibrational human beings, there was also a part of me that knew from all my personal development learnings that I did have to learn to forgive.

If I didn't forgive I would remain "stuck" in my pain, living a very mediocre life, and even worse, becoming bitter and twisted. This was not the life that I wanted to live, and this is not the life that you want to live either. Forgiveness is a crucial part of our healing and being able to move on with our lives.

It took me many years to adopt the power of forgiveness. Some of the things that I learned about forgiveness is that **you need to stop being so critical of yourself. You need to release the judgments and stop asking yourself all those WHY questions**. For example, "Why did I allow myself to get involved with this person?" "Why me?" "Why was I so stupid?" **Be very mindful of the questions you are asking yourself and make sure the conversations that you are having with yourself are not toxic and causing you further suffering.**

> *Practicing the art of forgiveness will change your life, as will being able to release so much suffering from your heart, enabling you to live so much more joyfully & peacefully*

Forgiveness and Healing

Forgiveness must be incorporated as part of your recovery and healing. Once you can forgive, you can then start to really live the life that you deserve, instead of being bogged down with "what ifs" and "should haves".

Be Your Own Source of Happiness

I do not recommend relying on your husband/partner and their family to be your entire life. **I strongly urge you need to create your**

own life, with your own friends, and your own interests, and doing things that YOU love. This is a must if you want to live a fulfilling life as your life is just as important.

In the event that your relationships go pear-shaped, and I sincerely hope they don't, at least you are **not** left with a completely empty life. **Regardless of whether you are in a relationship or single, we need to make the very most of our lives, and part of that is realising what drives you, what makes you happy, and what sets your heart and soul on fire.** If you have a partner and children, you may very well get a lot of joy from them, and that is great, but do not spend your entire life revolving around them and then wonder why you are not happy.

I have witnessed this often, and I have also been in the situation where I have done it. If you think about your life and wonder why you are not happy, it may be because it pretty much revolves around your partner, children, family and a job that you may not even like. This could be the very reason why you are feeling, complacent, exhausted, lacking drive and motivation.

You cannot live your life through someone else. You need to work out what your passions are, what your dreams are, and make sure they are also being fulfilled in some way, shape or form. Start making yourself a priority and do not lose sight of your own personal desires.

With regard to relationships, of course we never start a committed relationship thinking that it's going to end. Most of us think it is for life. The fact of the matter is, no matter how romantic you are, no matter how much you love your partner, and no matter how loyal and committed you may be, unexpected things can happen.

Life can sometimes take some very unexpected turns and for many reasons, relationships can fall apart. If you're currently in a relationship, I truly hope that it's very healthy, happy and loving, and that you stay together and therefore do not need to worry about how you may deal with a break-up.

Relationship separations and divorces are messy and painful under all circumstances; and if your life is empty because you didn't create your own life within the relationship, you will find it so much harder and excruciating until you rebuild it on your terms. It is a harsh lesson to learn, and won't be as painful if you have your own interests, friends and passions to fall back on.

Ho'oponopono

Ho'oponopono is a forgiveness practice that originated in Hawaii. It has tremendous healing abilities proven to be extremely powerful because of 4 statements repeated over and over. It is one of my most favourite "meditations" that I utilise and many versions can easily be found on YouTube where this practice is put to music.

For me, I personally I lay down on a bed, yoga mat or anywhere I am comfortable and warm, I shut my eyes and as I listen I repeat the four key healing statements:

I AM SORRY

PLEASE FORGIVE ME

I THANK YOU

AND I LOVE YOU

These are four of the most magically powerful statements that you could ever utilise to help you with the art of forgiveness, and I highly recommend this for you if you need to utilise forgiveness in your own life.

Prior to listening to this practice, write down a list of things that you think you need to forgive yourself for.

For me personally, I had a long list of things that required forgiveness. You may not, however, be clear on the things that you want to forgive yourself for. Once you have your list and a clear vision of what you want to release, choose the one thing that you want to work on prior to listening. Once the practice commences, you will know exactly what you need to work on in that moment.

Key Lessons:

- ❖ Stop beating yourself up and asking yourself "why me". Don't get "stuck" in your pain. Journal your feelings and release them on paper to assist you to get "unstuck".

- ❖ Surround yourself with supportive and inspirational people and avoid the toxic ones that don't support you.

- ❖ Be your own best friend and stop the judgments, harsh criticisms and negative self-talk. Be gentle and nurturing toward yourself.

- ❖ Forgive yourself and stop the blame game and negative self-talk.

- ❖ Lead a full and passionate life and do things that really set your heart and soul on fire – life is meant to be amazing.

- ❖ Make sure you are filling up your life with things and people that matter. Be more discriminating with your time, what you do and who you choose to spend it with. Remember that you are the master of your destiny and you are in charge of your own life.

- ❖ Do that "thing" that you have always wanted to do, but didn't because you always put your needs on hold. Learn a new skill, join a new group or workshop. Go on that retreat that you have always wanted to attend.

- ❖ Plan your financial future and make some tangible goals along with an action plan of what you need to do – prioritise your life. Dream big and start to create the life that you want, and one that is on your terms.
- ❖ Retain your sense of humour – watch comedies, go out with friends that are fun and entertaining and inspiring.

"In order to find stability in the world we must first find stability within ourselves"

– Tyler J Herbert

Lesson 9

You are Worthy of Stability

When I decided that my marriage was over, I started dating far too soon, and I didn't stop to contemplate my life or think about my actions. This was a pattern that I needed to change, but I was still too stuck in my pain to see this at the time.

I also started numbing myself out with shopping, sex and gambling. I had a brief affair with my gardener, only within a few weeks of my husband going to prison. It wasn't long before he was seducing me in my kitchen, taking me totally by surprise when he lunged at me and before I knew it, he had his head up my skirt. He had mastered the art of seduction that's for sure.

This ended up being a very expensive love affair, as he borrowed money from me and when I needed the cash back, he completely refused to pay and totally denied borrowing it in the first place. In hindsight, I should have transferred the money directly into his account, as then at least I would have had a record, or of course not lent the money in the first place!

I was starting to feel very isolated and I craved the city life once again. After a few months of dating a few different guys in Melbourne, and without too much thought, I decided to rent out my house on the Mornington Peninsula and move to a rented house in the inner north suburbs of Melbourne.

I loved the artistic vibe in our new inner-city home and all the wonderful array of restaurants, cafes and shops in the area. At the same time, I really did miss my own home, which I had lovingly restored and spent good money on refurbishing. The cottage that I had bought was transformed from something squatters would live in, to a beautiful home. I had put my heart and soul into that home and yet now I was renting a house in Melbourne that was not even renovated. It's hard to fathom what my thinking was, and I was certainly lacking stability in my life.

My estranged husband had been moved to a Victorian country prison that was mainly for sex offenders. After I decided I wanted a divorce, I knew I had to at least visit T and tell him face to face what my intentions were. I dreaded going to visit him in prison, and felt very uncomfortable confronting him, but I also knew it had to be done.

When I organised the visit and was face-to-face with him, T begged me not to divorce him, saying that he loved me so much and he needed my support. I told him very clearly that I could never trust him around my daughter, and there was no way that the marriage could continue. I recall him distinctly saying that other prisoner's wives visit them every week and have stood by their husbands, yet they have done far worse things to their daughters!

This was emotional manipulative behaviour at its finest – was it supposed to make me feel better about what he had done? T also tried to manipulate me by saying that I would be far better off financially if I stayed with him. Admittedly, I craved financial stability, however not at the expense of living a life with a child sexual offender and putting my daughter at risk – no money in the world was worth that.

A Whole New World to Contend With

My life had changed dramatically, as I had gone from what I thought was an amazing marriage and living a life of opulence, to walking into Centrelink for government benefits. I had no job or income, no husband and no real close friends that I could rely on to help and support me through this very difficult time.

I felt enormous grief and deep isolation from the rest of the world, and at times I felt like it was my daughter and I against the world. I was drowning in those early days of single motherhood and was completely unconsciously sabotaging my happiness. The next relationship was going to be one of the most horrific that I would ever experience. This particular relationship would take years to release the guilt and the shame and be able to heal completely from the whole wretched experience.

Meeting the Conman

My husband would still ring me from time to time to check in and see how my daughter and I were going. I think he was still wishing and hoping we would get back together. My husband had made friends with this guy named M#2 and they had apparently become best buddies. There were a few conversations where he put his buddy M#2 on the phone. M#2 was **not** a child sex offender, but had been convicted on fraud and deception charges (big red flag!).

Suddenly M#2 started calling me frequently and writing me amazing letters. He continuously romanced me with his words and I even started looking forward to his calls. *I will add at this point, to this day I still don't know if it was him who actually wrote the letters. I also do not know whether my husband had deliberately orchestrated M#2 and I getting together.* My family certainly had their suspicions.

I built my relationship with M#2 from phone calls and letters. We wrote to each other often and even though I hadn't ever met him, I was so drawn to him; his voice, his charm and the ease of conversation was so very compelling. Even over the phone, M#2 seemed very magnetic and he had such a sexy voice.

I also remember thinking to myself, "Yes this guy is a convicted criminal, however nothing could be worse than a child sex offender". He also started promising me the world, and because I was so emotionally vulnerable and so very naive and idealistic, I believed everything that he told me.

The Affair with the Conman

M#2 spoke about all his investments and how he was looking forward to getting out of prison and living the life of luxury once again. He said that he was falling in love with me and he kept saying that he wished that one day we could be together. He also told me I deserved to be with someone who wasn't a sex offender. This was the start of his "con job" on me.

Eventually I got to meet M#2 when he was transferred to another lower security prison. I felt his magnetism over the phone, but to meet him in person after months of phone conversations and letters was a whole other level. When we finally met each other for the first time, the attraction was instant and it was very mutual. I remember he commented on how lovely I dressed, and how I was far sexier than my husband had portrayed me. The endless compliments, promises and his declaration of his love for me was intensified at this time.

I would visit M#2 every weekend until he was released. Just prior to Christmas, he put in a big shopping list of all the things he wanted. That in itself should have been a warning sign as who does that? However, I naively went out and bought everything on that list. I was always very generous with the people that I cared about, and he was certainly taking advantage of my generosity.

We even got engaged and started planning our lives prior to his release. I really thought I loved this man and this was my chance to rebuild my life. He told me to start looking for prestigious properties for purchase, as his property was being rented for another 12 months. I naively started researching properties, and went to the extent of choosing a private school in an amazing area for my daughter to attend.

After approximately eight months of weekend visits, I picked him up on his release day, and initially we lived in my rented home in the inner northern suburbs of Melbourne. It wasn't long before he convinced me to put my house on the market even though it was currently tenanted.

He was a cunning man and he knew my gorgeous cottage would sell much easier if we moved back to the property. This is exactly what I stupidly did, and we moved back in with all my beautiful furnishings, and within weeks my house had sold. At the time, he also convinced me to sell my car, on the pretence that he had ordered me a new Mercedes and that I would have it within the next few months and that we temporarily required the cashflow.

I had never in my life encountered a con man and I was the sort of person who very stupidly took people by their word. It was a very harsh lesson to realise that not everyone is to be trusted, and there are people who are extremely deceptive.

Many of my family and friend's lives were affected financially as well, and many were very unhappy with me and blamed me for what had happened. I was the one who brought this man into their lives, and even though I had nothing to do with his deception, it did not stop some of them blaming me.

Some of my family relationships would become very strained, and when I needed their emotional support, I was not able to receive it because they were so caught up in dealing with their financial losses, they found it difficult to understand how much I was manipulated and controlled by M#2.

You know those current affair programs that highlight nasty conmen? Well, unfortunately he was one of those. Just when I thought my life couldn't get any worse, my life was really was about to hit rock bottom, as I had put my trust and love into a relationship with a horrible, abusive, and controlling conman.

Without even realising at the time, I was going to create a life that was extremely unstable and I will go onto to explain exactly why in my next chapter. I truly was going to have to connect to a place deep within and know that I was worthy of stability and stop the sabotage and this pattern of destruction behaviour.

Your Path to Stability

Your path to stability can be a long road if you have been brought up feeling insecure, anxious, or with an upbringing that was unstable. Part of your sub-conscious has a much greater chance of creating more instability, if you have negative childhood conditioning.

It is only **when you become conscious of your life** that you can change and in turn create a stable life. For many of us, this is not an automatic response and we have to clear a lot of our negative beliefs before we can really create a life that is stable.

Stability can mean different things to different people; however, I am talking about stability in your career/job, relationships, health and your overall behaviour. Creating more peace in your heart, not running away from problems and not sabotaging your good relationships or attracting the toxic ones, is a great path to creating your stability.

Awareness is one the keys and then making the necessary positive changes to your behaviour, so that you do not continue down a path of instability. Do not become the "master of instability" like I did. Make the changes that are for your highest good only and start to create a stable life and know that you are worthy of a better life.

Using Addictions to Numb the Pain

If you honestly think about your life do you think you have used an addiction to numb out your pain? There are many types of addictions, including alcohol, drugs, gambling, shopping, sex or food. If you have been numbing your pain with any form of addiction, there is every chance that you have been living a life that is unconscious and mediocre in some way.

When we are dealing with enormous trauma it can be very difficult to deal with our feelings, so for many of us we use some form of addiction to numb out our pain as we think it is an easier path.

For me it was a combination of sex, food, shopping, and the worst addiction was going to become my gambling.

If I had stopped to think about my behaviour, maybe I would have **sought help** and would have made better decisions, **created some solid boundaries** and accessed some of my buried **wisdom and personal development practices**. There was a short period of time that I did go to some Gamblers Anonymous meetings, and during the time I attended these meetings I did stop gambling. However, it was short-lived, instead I continued to numb myself out instead of dealing with my buried emotions which were still unconsciously causing me pain.

Addictions can take a long time to recover from and I am not even sure if you ever fully recover, you just adapt your behaviour. I now avoid anything to do with gambling, as I still worry that I may lose my control and use it as a mechanism to deal with my stress during a weak moment. I think the key here is to live an amazing life, one that is balanced, one that is full of joy and passion, so you don't really have the need to gamble any longer.

When you are in a state of being emotionally destructive, it can be really difficult to even recognise that you need to change and that you need help. This becomes a major problem in itself, and — of course — hindsight is a wonderful thing, as it's much easier to see clearly after tragic events what you may have done differently.

People in your life that have not experienced what you have, will not quite understand and they may say things like "Why did you do this or that?". This is not helpful, as during these times you need support, understanding and compassion. You certainly do not need other people's judgments and criticisms, as you are no doubt, very good at doing that yourself.

My gambling journey started very innocently, and at first it was something my first husband, T and I did when we went on holidays, mainly to interstate locations where there were Casinos. We would save for our holiday and put away extra money for gambling and spending. I would never gamble on the horses at this point in time, unless it was the Spring Carnival. I never went near the poker machines and in actual fact, I hated them as they seemed so very boring and a waste of time.

It wasn't until T went to jail that I increased my gambling at the Casino and then started regularly going to the TAB. It was no surprise when I became involved with M#2 who loved gambling, that he would completely use this against me. Believe me, it didn't look very good when I gambled with him, as in true stereo-typed conman style, M#2 was gambling with other people's money, including my own.

Of course, I stupidly thought M#2 was legitimately wealthy and was going to pay everyone back, including myself! I didn't realise it at the time, but M#2 had deliberately set me up to look like I was also conning people. When M#2 left me practically penniless, I suffered deep depression, and I started to gamble even more excessively. I even started playing those dreaded pokies for the very first time and that horrid slippery-slope of my gambling addiction would take on a whole new level.

These machines are set up to entice us and numb us out so that we lose all sense of reality. **I remember when I gambled, I felt no pain and it was like I was in a completely different world – it was a complete illusion.** If you observe people gambling at many of the venues you may notice how lonely, sad and disconnected they look. Towards the end of my gambling addiction, I would put myself in that category. I was one of those very sad and desperate individuals.

Recognise the signs

An obvious sign when you have a gambling addiction is that you become utterly obsessed with it and have a deep need to want to gamble every single day. You find that you are constantly thinking about it, your thoughts are consumed with how you can gamble during the course of your day, even when you are working. You start losing concentration and becoming quite agitated.

Another sign that your out of control, would be that when gambling, you lose total track of the time and start to become robotic, continuously going to the ATM until you have exceeded your daily limit. You even temporarily forget that it it's real money! If you can relate to this, I would then say that you have a gambling addiction, but I am not expert and this is just my journey. Do not assume because so many other people are gambling and it seems a "sociable" thing to do that it is okay. If you actually stop and reflect and ask yourself "is this behaviour really for my highest good" and "Am I out of control, but just don't want to admit it"?

Get help as soon as possible before your gambling addiction gets any worse and you end up either broke, alone or both. Please stop being in denial.

You need to know that you deserve to live a much healthier amazing and "stable" life and not one wasted on spending time gambling away your hard-earned cash and becoming a "zombie". There will be days when you will win, and it will be the best adrenalin shot, especially when you win big amounts. I had quite a few of these moments and in the early days I remember being at the Casino and winning a $23,000 jackpot. I bought a new car for cash, took my daughter on a luxurious Gold Coast holiday, and paid off my credit cards. It was a such a huge high and a moment that I will never forget as soon as I knew I had won the jackpot.

The problem is the chances of you winning another jackpot are probably very slim; however, it's like you crave to have that adrenalin rush once again. For me, there were a few other big wins and the only way that I could replace these amazing feelings was to eventually fall more in love with my life and get high from leading a vibrant passionate & purposeful life.

The flip side to remember, is the disgust, regret and sick feeling in your stomach when you lose and have gone through so much of your money. I suggest that you hold that feeling and remember it every time you feel the need to gamble. Please do not stick your head in the sand for many years like I did waste your, time, money and your life away. Get the help you need now so you can create a happier, more magnificent and stable existence.

Please stop and think about what you are doing and what habits you may have formed because of your pain. The questions may be:

- Am I gambling too much or am I using an addiction to mask and/or numb my pain?
- Am I attracting terrible relationships?
- Am I really dealing with my suffering or am I pretending everything is ok?

Sex to Numb the Pain

I also created a distinct pattern throughout my life when it came to a lot of my sexual encounters. I had always thought that I was healthy when it came to my sexuality, and thought that sex was a wonderfully pleasurable act to enjoy. I personally feel it's great to be sexually liberated and not be hung up about your sexuality and taking on shame or guilt. It becomes extremely unhealthy when we are using sex as a means of numbing out our pain, like I was doing at times.

Becoming Conscious

The worst thing you can do when dealing with your suffering is to become completely unconscious. If you do react in this way, you will most likely continue to live a life that is not "deliciously divine". You may also prevent yourself from being healed as you will not realise just how much pain you are carrying at a subconscious level.

When you heal, when you start to believe in yourself and increase your self-worth, you will slowly but surely start to understand that you deserve so much more than living an existence that is mediocre. It's time for you to really wake-up and for you to become fully conscious of your life.

Do not continue to go down the slippery slope of addiction. Stop, pause, think – then put a plan in place for how you can improve your life and once again return to joy, love and peace and stability. You are so worthy of this and so much more!

Key Lessons:

- ❖ Look after yourself and nurture yourself even more after a relationship break-up. This is the time to really look after yourself and become healthier so you can become more resilient.

- ❖ Invest in yourself – personal development, read, research, attend courses/seminars/retreats. Really work on improving yourself.

- ❖ Know that you are completely worth a stable existence. This could be in regards to work, relationships, your home-life etc.

- ❖ Become conscious of your life so that you can make clearer decisions and do not make big life decisions when you are emotions are still very raw and your "stuck" your pain.

- ❖ Avoid numbing out your pain with addictions as avoidance and filling the void. As much as it is painful be real about how you are feeling and utilise techniques to help you through your suffering.

- ❖ Realise that sex can be healthy and be pleasurable, however be mindful if you are using sex to numb out your pain.

- ❖ Get professional counselling/therapy to help specifically with your addictive behaviour.
- ❖ Find tools to be able to increase your self-worth and self-love so you can make better choices. Fill up your life with people and pursuits that you love and start to honour & cherish you and your time.
- ❖ Stop trying to find happiness from others and seek from within yourself.
- ❖ Connect to your heart and soul and create regular self-care practices and rituals & meditation to allow this to happen.
- ❖ Be honest with yourself and how you are living your life, even asking yourself those difficult questions.

"Abundance is not something we acquire, it is something we tune into"
— Wayne Dyer

Lesson 10

You Are Worthy of Abundance

Unfortunately, my life was going to get a lot worse than just losing my financial security. I also had to admit to myself and my family that we had all been conned, although I discovered later on that my family knew this far before I did. The fact that M#2 was a deceitful conman was bad enough, but he took it to a whole new level, as he was also very abusive and controlling.

As mentioned, M#2 encouraged me to stop renting my house and for us to move back to my cottage, as this was part of his deceitful plan to access the remaining money from the sale of the house. In true conman fashion, he promised that it was a temporary loan and I would get everything back.

You know the old story you have probably heard a million times before about how common it is for a professional conman to behave like this. But let me tell you, when you are actually involved with someone as cunning, manipulative and convincing as M#2 it's amazing what you believe.

He was even able to convince me to purchase a $33,000 Holden Statesman Caprice for him, which only a few weeks later we had to sell for substantially less to pay back some of his debts. It was at this time when family members had become quite suspicious of him and demanded their initial investment back, unfortunately only to be conned again by him. He was the "master of manipulation and deceit"!

The Abusive Conman

Just prior to the settlement of my home, M#2 conveniently found a beach house in a very prestigious part of the Mornington Peninsula, so I stupidly paid six month's rent in advance on this property. M#2 cunning plan was to keep me very isolated from most of my friends and family members, live in luxury and pretend to everyone he was rich. Little did they know he was either living off me or all the other people he was ripping off.

I still naively thought that he was the man I would spend the rest of my life with. This was until the unthinkable happened, when he raped me in every way possible: sexually, physically, emotionally, and financially.

He was quickly becoming a fierce bully who would verbally abuse me and also physically assault me daily. The physical abuse was not in an obvious way, or the kind that would leave bruises on my face, as he would not have wanted to create attention. He would often simply walk past me and pinch me incredibly hard to the point of me practically being in tears as it hurt so much. The worst part of the physical abuse was yet to come, it would be the sexual rape.

For many years I had flashbacks of when this happened, and I still shudder at the thought that I could get involved with such a beast. It was in the last few weeks of our relationship that he anally raped me on my sofa one night without any real warning. He was like an unhinged animal pouncing on me and then pushing me onto my tummy and slamming into me with such force. He had cleverly put me in such a position that I could not escape from him and he was quite a solid man. I had never had this type of sex before, so it was extremely brutal and very unexpected. I was actually in shock that he could even take his bullying and aggressiveness to such extremities.

It took me many years to even talk about the rape, and it wasn't until a few years ago that I realised I was still holding onto the shame of it. It was at this point I needed to go even deeper with my healing and give myself permission to release it fully. I also had to forgive myself for ever allowing such a disgusting human being to be part of my inner sanctuary.

It was after the sexual rape that I finally began to question his love for me and his sincerity. Wow was I that slow to realise just what a brut he was! I was also feeling so ashamed that I could be controlled and abused in every way. It was one of the lowest points in my life, where I felt utterly helpless, worthless, and very much alone.

How could any man that truly loved me contemplate raping me and in such a harsh way? He was a controlling abusive and manipulative beast! This was the man I thought was my second chance and the man I thought I would marry and share a dream life with. Believe me this was no dream; it was a living bloody nightmare. He also raped me financially, to the point of near bankruptcy and he raped me emotionally, pretending to love me, pretending to want to marry me, and all along just wanting to deceive me.

After "ripping me off" to the point where I had no assets left, as my house, my car and anything of value had been sold, he became even more controlling and abusive. I was totally allowing him to control my life and I actually believed his stupid lies. I had gone from a financially secure independent woman, to someone who no longer made any decisions for herself, felt isolated, controlled, and was now broke. My self-worth was non-existent.

Because of the enormity and intensity of my situation, a huge part of me was hanging on thinking all would be okay, and that he couldn't possibly be lying. He couldn't possibly be a conman. It must have also been the fear of him that kept me imprisoned and compelled to stay with him at this time. I felt trapped and worthless with no self-confidence, with little strength and I felt like a complete failure.

I was very naive, had completely lost my way and was blinded by his deceptive behaviour. My judgements and decisions were beyond terrible! It's only now I understand that when a woman is being abused and controlled, she has completely given away her power and has very little self-worth, her mind is not clear and she can become paralysed with fear. When you are put in a situation like this and experiencing such abuse, it's very easy to be completely blind to your actual situation.

He must have thought I was such easy prey, as I loved gambling and he could smell my vulnerability. He also saw big dollar signs. I imagine my ex-husband telling him about all our Casino adventures and the large amounts of cash we used to gamble. The biggest difference with M#2's gambling was that it was a massive sickness, to the point he had become a criminal to finance his habit.

It was also such a clever plan of his to associate with a fellow gambler, then blame me and utilise my credibility to get to others. He was one very sick individual who would go to extremes to get what he wanted, with no thought or care of the people he affected. He was a nasty piece of well-rehearsed work. He had a way of convincing people to believe his outlandish stories, and that they would all get their money back.

After nine months of him being released from prison, it would be revealed that M#2 had no money whatsoever. He just gambled away everyone else's and never had any intentions of paying anyone back. He would continue to lie, deceive, and cheat people as long as he could get away with it. Eventually people became wise to his antics, but only when it was far too late to stop his destruction, although I was one of the last people to understand exactly what type of person he was.

I never kept it a secret from my family that I was dating a convicted criminal. I remember my Mum warning me, and saying to me that he had been charged with fraud and to please be careful. She also said that for my age, I was a reasonably wealthy woman, as I owned my house and had no debts.

Mum knew how vulnerable I was emotionally, and that I was not in a good state of mind to be able to make wise decisions. My mother never trusted him or believed his BS. Mothers have an inbuilt intuition, especially when it comes to their own children. It's a pity we often do not listen to our Mums, and we instead choose to take the difficult path!

My mother was absolutely right not to trust him, as she could see that I was getting to the stage where I was running out of money and anything of any value was sold on the proviso that he would buy me a car, repay all the cash and buy multiple houses when his money came through. Not to mention he also promised to replace all my beautiful antiques that he had sold.

My family began to realise that he was a conman, and they were fearing the worst —that they would never get their money back. They had been completed fooled by M#2 and he had devised a cunning plan to deceive anyone he met, including some of my very close family members. It's bad enough that he had ripped me off financially (not to mention all the abuse that I received) but to con my family as well, amplified my pain greatly.

I know many will judge me for being completely stupid and gullible, and even dating a criminal in the first place. Add into the mix that I had my beautiful 4- year old daughter to protect and look after. I felt a miserable failure as a mother at this time in my life.

I do want to express at this point, that unless you have been to the pits of despair, and in particular been in an abusive relationship, you may not understand how good people make really bad judgements. We were also dealing with a seasoned professional conman who had ripped off many people in his past and he was exceptionally good at what he did.

I also feel unless you have suffered huge loss, betrayal, depression and given away your power and felt so worthless and vulnerable, you may not understand how I could be so "stupid". If you have also felt these emotions, you will understand how I felt, and how much we can lose our way and make such terrible decisions.

I knew that I had a huge amount of work to do on myself, as I unfortunately had not connected with or utilised any of my inner-wisdom and my teachings for such a long time. How would I move forward from these traumas? How could I stop sabotaging my happiness, including my financial security? How could I trust myself with my decision making? How could I rebuild my life? I had no choice but to start again and I knew I couldn't just give up on my life. For the sake of myself and my daughter, I had to dig deeper for extra courage and resilience to re-build both our lives.

It was 1998, and approximately a month prior to Christmas, and I was now living with my mother and my step-father in their small two-bedroom unit, sharing a bedroom with my daughter. I had no house, no car, no job, no relationship, no close friends, estranged with some family members, many debts and a heart that felt like it had been ripped apart. I also now know that I buried the whole rape incident and the pain and torment resided in my whole being as I had not released it or healed from this abuse – numbing out was my unhealthy way of coping. My saving grace at this time was my daughter and the love that I received from my mother.

I found out later the ugly truth that M#2 knew the police were after him and he had deliberately left to escape them whilst we were living at the beachside house. He had basically cleaned me out financially anyway, so in his eyes I wasn't much good to him any longer. He had successfully completed his mission of destroying my life in most ways, and he had done a stellar job.

Between the sex offender husband and then meeting and trusting a conman/rapist, you would think I would have given up all hope on love. I didn't know how but I was determined to rebuild my disastrous life. There were some really dark days, but I knew that I had to keep going and that I couldn't give up, not for me or for the sake of my daughter.

I had to find a way out of this big, dark, black hole and I wasn't about to give in easily. There was, no doubt, a long journey ahead, and at times things seemed so bleak. It was an effort to create any form of normality and balance in my life, let alone once again live in joy. I had to answer some tough questions, including: why did I not think that I was worthy of abundance and why was I sabotaging my happiness?

Your Path to Abundance

Abundance comes in all forms, and everyone has the same chances to connect to abundance. I think that many people allow fear to stop them from connecting to abundance, allowing themselves to stay in a scarcity mentality and in turn self-sabotage.

The only difference between someone who is abundant and someone who is not, is that the abundant are not connecting to fear. They comprehend that consciously, or even sub-consciously, abundance is all around us, and each and every one of us has the potential to connect to it.

> *"We don't create abundance. Abundance is always present.*
> *We create limitations."*
> *—Arnold Patent*

One of the key steps to creating a path to abundance is that we need to break our old negative conditioning. We also need to believe, create and then put in the action so we can connect to abundance. We need to begin appreciating that there is an unlimited and infinite universal supply for all. This includes amazing health, wealth, absolute happiness, peace and love.

Abundance can also relate to having a great sense of self-worth and knowing that you are completely worthy of living an abundant life. It's often when we have low self-worth that we can become our own worst enemies and can stay stuck in our lower vibration. Once we raise our vibration and we allow the abundance into our lives, this I believe is the game-changer.

Healing

When you begin the healing process is when you are on the right path to creating abundance. When you realise that you are deserving, you will stop playing small and your victim mentality will become less and less, allowing you to connect to more abundance. When you acknowledge your suffering, that is when you can get really serious about healing from it. For anyone like myself who has been abused, we know that the memory never leaves us. We may bury the memory for a while but it will affect our lives in so many ways until we allow ourselves to be healed.

For anyone who has been abused in any way, I send you so much love and healing and I want you to know deep down in your soul that you were not deserving of any form of abuse and that you deserve an amazing and abundant life.

Give yourself this permission and forgive yourself for allowing any form of suffering to have occurred in the first place. I know how extremely painful this process can be, but I also know that once we are able to allow ourselves to heal from our suffering, our lives can change miraculously.

I found that working through the powerful principles of forgiveness and healing, eventually meant that I could move on from my own suffering and begin to make better choices, have healthier relationships and become far more abundant. It's through my journey that I also know that it is possible for you to move on and that you can live a fabulous life once again. You owe it to yourself to being your best version of you in this lifetime.

> *"My past has not defined me, destroyed me,*
> *deterred me, or defeated me"*
> *– Steve Maroboli*

Make it your mission in life to not allow your past to define you, destroy, deter or defeat you. When you can flip this around to surrendering, creating and being victorious, is when you will marvel at how wonderful and abundant your life truly can be.

We can all go through extreme suffering but the difference is what we learn from these harsh lessons and how we move forward in life.

We all have a choice, so choose wisely and don't ever think that you cannot achieve magnificence in your life.

Work on Your Financial Blocks:

I believe one of the ways to work on your financial blocks and to clear conditioning from your childhood is to invest in deep healing. Allow yourself to clear not only your present pain, but change that old movie in your mind too, and those silly lies that you tell yourself. I feel that if you do not clear this old conditioning, you will continue to block your abundance, including building and retaining your wealth.

What Past Conditioning Do You Need to Clear?

For me, I remember my Dad constantly saying *"Money does not bring you happiness"* and also *"Money does not grow on trees"*. I know people who have been told negative statements about money, which have then been ingrained in their minds, sometimes consciously and sometimes unconsciously. Because of this conditioning we can become irresponsible with money, which may include spending above your means, not having a regular savings plan and being reckless when it comes to the money that you earn.

Someone very close to me had a mother who had said to him for many years, *"you're shit with money"*. He took that statement completely to heart, and continued to lose his money, including making very bad investments and also spending his money frivolously, even though he earned a great income.

He was determined to prove his mother right instead of wrong. He was like me in that he was also someone able to manifest money, but not retain it. In his case it was a slightly different old dialogue that kept playing out in his mind. This is how a self-professing prophecy can play out in your life. **Never forget how powerful our minds are so feed your mind with positive reaffirming**

statements. We really need to clear that old conditioning to really more forward and retain your abundance.

I firmly believe we can break the negative conditioning from our childhoods no matter how entrenched it may be. This is why the only thing that will get between you connecting to abundance in your life is your own mind and your personal belief system. Once you utilise the fundamentals of personal development and start reprogramming that powerful mind of yours, you will experience amazing changes.

Are you Afraid of Success?

You may have been surrounded with people who did not believe in you, people who laughed at your dreams, like I was when growing up. I also found that I would attract some successes and then would find that people would distance themselves from me or be threatened by my little wins, rather than be excited and supportive.

I was still dealing with being a "people-pleaser", so I would retract back and I actually found it easier **not** to become successful. I was afraid of success, as I had associated it with being disliked, and I so wanted to be accepted and liked.

Dream Big Regardless

Being a people-pleaser and having a constant need to be accepted can have a profound effect on you, and can really reduce your abundance in so many ways. Most of us want to be "accepted" by our family and our closest friends, to the point where we will even block some amazing things in our life, thinking that this will help us to be more accepted.

If you can relate to this, then it's time for you to clear that "people pleaser" part of yourself. Remember to do YOU, then the right people will like and love you. Do not continue to live a "smaller" life thinking more people will like and accept you. The right people will like you and they will celebrate your success. Stay focussed and on your own path.

Replacing negative patterns and not allowing other people or difficult circumstances to prevent you from your dreams is necessary, if you truly want to lead a magnificent life. The more we love and honour ourselves, the less we will be inclined to do this. I have personally found it to be easier as I have gotten older, and I refuse to tolerate other people's BS for the sake of fitting in and being liked. This was a challenge, but I knew I needed to be able to do this for the sake of my own happiness.

> *"What others think of you is none of your business"*
> *– Jack Canfield*

Be totally accountable for your own life – stop the blame game. If you really want to live an abundant life, you must continue on your path, regardless of your conditioning, regardless of your terrible childhood, your horrible ex's or family, or the negative dialogue of your friends.

You must realise that you are the master of your destiny and you are totally in charge and in control of your life. If you are still blaming other people for a life that is not where you want it to be then stop, and start to be fully accountable. Not being accountable could block your abundance and so will any negative behavioural patterns and toxic mindsets. Reprogram your mind and reprogram your life if it is not where you want it to be.

> *Commit to change, commit to consciousness and commit to your life. Become your own master of commitment toward YOU and commit to living the best life possible*

Many of us can become a master at manifesting and then sabotage everything we have manifested. Have you attracted money, only to lose it or give it away? You may also need to have a good, long hard look at your inner thoughts on money and look back to your childhood for some clues as to why you would behave the way you do. Some of these clues may be because you grew up with phrases like:

- ❖ *"Money doesn't grow on trees"*
- ❖ *"Money doesn't buy happiness"*
- ❖ *"Money is the root of all evil"*
- ❖ *"Rich people are bastards"*
- ❖ *"You are shit with money"*

If you do not clear this old conditioning, there is every chance that you will continue to sabotage your financial security and abundance.

The bottom line is if you do not think you are worthy, abundance will either not be given to you in the first place, or if you are like me, it will be taken from you and sometimes in the most tragic of circumstances.

Know your own worth and know that you are completely worthy of abundance.

It is very wise to invest in yourself and in your personal development as you are your biggest investment. Continually work on your self-worth, so that you not only attract, **but retain abundance**. Clear your money blocks, in particular old conditioning that has hung around for far too long, limiting your success and abundance. It's time to release all that is weighing you down, and it's time to step up, believe in yourself, and know you are worthy of abundance.

Create an Abundant Mentality

Having or creating an abundant mentality is crucial if you are going to make any real changes in your life. You need to choose your words carefully as our minds our like mini-computers. Our minds do not know the difference between fact or fiction, so if you feed your mind with positive and inspiring thoughts and you consistently use this type of language when you are communicating, you will "trick" your mind into believing it is true.

If you feed your mind with negative self-talk and communicate in a self-defeating way, you are already setting yourself up for a life that is not abundant. Our minds are very powerful so don't underestimate the power of your thoughts – make sure they are positive and **not** self-defeating and toxic.

Choose your Thoughts Wisely and utilise empowering beliefs over limiting beliefs

Here is an example below of the difference in language and thought processes: (Author unknown)

Limiting Beliefs versus Empowering beliefs:

Limiting Beliefs	**Empowering Beliefs**
I am a victim of my circumstances	I create my own reality
Life happens to me	Life happens for me
I live in scarcity there is never enough	I live in abundance and there is always enough
Obstacles hold me back	Obstacles help me grow and learn
I cannot do that until ____happens	Starting before you are ready leads to success
This is too hard – I should quit	If it were easy everyone else would be doing it

When you choose empowering language over limiting language, your life will change. Changing your negative thought processes and your language will have a huge impact on improving your life.

A letter to you: It is time to create abundance

Dear Beautiful one,

It's time to realise that you can be as abundant as

anyone else and that it is your right

It's time to feel the fear and do it anyway

It's time to stop worrying about insignificant stuff

It's time to stop the comparisons

It's time to stop the self-sabotage

It's time to stop the negative self-talk

It's time to stop numbing out your pain

It's time to not waste another day in scarcity

It's time to ask for guidance and support

When you have lost your way

It's time to heal, to forgive and to trust again

It's time to be grateful for everything that you do have

And realise the more grateful you are the more you will

have to be grateful for

It's time to open your arms wide and graciously accept

Everything that is for your highest good

It's time to trust the flow of the universe and know

it has your back

It's time to realise your worth

It's time to honour and value who you are

It's time to get really clear on what you do want

It's time to visualise and affirm the EXACT life

That you want to create

It's time to see it

It's time to feel it

It's time to taste it

It's time to shout out "I have got this and I am

so deserving"!

It's time

It's most definitely your time

To live an abundant and amazing life

So much love & abundance

Jo Worthy

"Nothing is more important than reconnecting with your bliss. Nothing is as rich. Nothing is more real"

– Deepak Chopra

Lesson 11

You are Worthy of Bliss

After a few weeks of living with my Mum and stepdad, I was very fortunate that my beautiful grandmother was able to help me financially, so that I could set up my own place for my daughter and I. I found a home that was just around the corner from my mother and step-father, which allowed them to be such a great support. We both certainly needed that extra love, support and encouragement during this very difficult time in our lives.

The absolute joy in my heart that I felt to have a home once again for my precious daughter and I was huge. I was grateful that I still had some lovely furnishings and that I was still able to make a very comfortable home. This home may have been very humble, but it was one that I could fill with love and beauty. Even more importantly, both my daughter and I were free from the abusive evil conman.

I have tears in my eyes as I write this, as I remember having so much gratitude in my heart for the help that I received. I now felt that I could move on from the abuse, the deception and the trauma that I had experienced over the previous few years. There was still some hope and some light that I could draw on and it's times like this in our lives where we need to feel grateful for everything that we do have, not what we don't have.

Count Your Blessings, Not Your Losses

I also felt blessed that I was able to get my daughter into the local school as she was due to start in a few months. Additionally, it wasn't that long after moving into our new home that I got a job, and it was extremely important to me that I was able to provide not only a home, but also to be in a position that I could pay all the household bills, buy good quality food, and still provide a good life.

I felt lucky that my daughter settled into school so well and she actually loved it. This was a huge relief to me as I wanted her to feel safe, secure and happy once again. After coming out of such a toxic and abusive relationship, you cannot help but feel guilt towards bringing someone so terrible into not only your own life, but your child's. To be honest, it still saddens me that my judgement was so poor, although with the healing and the power of forgiveness and gratitude, my guilt has lessened dramatically.

I made friends with quite a few of the mothers within the community, which really helped me to settle into our new life. We continued lovely friendships for quite a few years and thank heavens for my girlfriends in those days. We enjoyed quite a few nights at each other's homes, laughing and chatting over a glass of wine, and they were really lovely down-to-earth genuine women. With what I was dealing with emotionally, I don't think they realised how much I needed and appreciated their friendship.

It was only after the fiasco with M#2 that I would once again draw on the basic fundamentals of visualisations and affirmations to help get my life back in order and be able to attract some of the things that we often take for granted.

Having a car was one of the things that maybe I did take for granted, until I had to take two buses and a train to work. Miraculously, I obtained a car loan, and was able to get another car, similar to the one M#2 sold. It was a Honda Prelude which was the car that I had been visualising for a few months.

When your belief is unwavering, the miracles will occur

Dreams do come true when we believe and then take the necessary action, accompanied with gratitude. It is such a powerful combination. The fact that I was able to get another car so that I didn't have to spend over 1.5 hours getting to work, could run my daughter around, plus go grocery shopping, was such a huge gift to me from the universe.

I had made a firm agreement with myself that I would not continue to live in suffering, lack, or have a scarcity mentality. Under my circumstances, it would have been very easy to remain a victim and adopt a more negative and limiting mindset. My new mantra quickly became "**I do not do poverty**".

Single Motherhood

Becoming a single mother was never on my "wish list" and it's certainly not for the faint hearted, but you do learn to be resourceful and you become extremely resilient and humble. Even in the pits of my despair, I look back and I am surprised by the amount of courage and determination I displayed. This was despite the numbing out and many moments of being in denial, I did have many moments where I displayed huge amounts of resilience.

With my first husband going off to prison in November 1995, was my first experience of becoming a single mother. Even though my life at the time, could only be described as shattered into a million pieces, I had to dig deep, keep going, and live a life not only for my sake, but also for my daughter.

Even though if the truth be known, I was drowning in grief and some of my days were very dark, to avoid too many of the "dark" days my coping mechanism was to numb out my emotions. **Pure avoidance is not recommended – we cannot heal from our pain if we are constantly in denial –** I was to learn this the hard way!

The world of gambling

As mentioned, I had been introduced to a world of gambling with my ex-husband and it had become a significant part of our social life as well. When he went to prison, a huge part of me was still attracted to this world and I would get all glammed up and go off to the Casino, when I wasn't working, or even in my lunch hour if I was working. At the time, I actually thought it was a great life and the frequent visits to the Casino became my escape from reality and my only form of a "social" life.

At this time my social life was limited due to being a single parent and I wanted to spend evenings at home with my daughter. I wanted to create some normality for my daughter, with home-cooked meals and movie nights. Routine and structure at home with my daughter was important. However, the regular gambling during the day when my daughter was at school became a very negative behavioural pattern, and one which I didn't really talk about to other people.

Occasionally, when I actually thought about my life, I felt very foolish and very regretful. The betrayal, the lies and the deception I had experienced from my past two relationships, if I thought about it for too long, would make me sick to my very core. When I was gambling, I forgot about my pain which seemed like a blessing at the time, but of course it was far from that…

It was not a healthy existence and I was NOT utilising any of my personal development learnings. I was on a path of destruction and was completely out of flow and out of sync with the universe. I never really hesitated, stopped to breathe, or thought about what I was going to do with my life and what I wanted to achieve. I was going through the motions of just trying to keep it together, but really drowning in grief underneath.

Forgiveness

Forgiveness was going to become a major component to enable me to move on with my life in many ways, along with releasing a lot of that "shame shit" so that it would not hold me back for the rest of my life and prevent me from being the very best version of myself. Many of us make a lot of mistakes, some make a few, however we all make them. In my case I just happened to make a lot of them, so the journey of forgiving myself was going to take some time, and it would take a lot longer than I ever anticipated.

Stop Living a Mediocre Life

Upon the realisation that the best thing I could do for my daughter was to heal and in turn create a healthy lifestyle for us both - I had to stop living a half-baked life, and I had to stop making terrible judgements when it came to allowing certain people into my life. Living a half-baked life is not a life – it's like you're living half a life, and walking around half dead.

I am afraid for those first few years after my husband went to prison, I was like a robot just going through the motions. I still believe, to this day, that's why I attracted such deceptive people into my life. Not only was I emotionally vulnerable, I was also an "open vessel" for attracting people with such a low vibration! Also, I believe because my own self-love was non-existent, **this enabled me to attract such toxic relationships in the first place**.

To the outside world I did not want to be seen as a needy, stupid woman who couldn't make a wise decision to save herself. Although the truth of the matter was that is exactly how I felt underneath the veil. This was regardless of the polite smiles, the "fake" confidence, the lovely clothes and the "no one will ever fuck me over again" attitude. I actually felt like the biggest idiot on this planet, and my confidence and trust was completely shattered.

I didn't feel proud of my choices or the men that I had attracted which took me to a whole new level of feeling like a failure. I had massive personal work to do and if I didn't do the work, I would most likely completely drown in my own idiotic thoughts and self-loathing. I was already drowning so I needed a "life boat" to save me and I needed one quickly. I was on a search so that my life could become blissful once again.

Your Path to Creating Bliss

A huge part of our purpose in life is to consciously create a life that is blissful, not one that is full of regrets, doubts, fears and turmoil. I recommend that you become fully conscious and create your own "master life plan". Your "master plan" can include quotes, affirmations, visualisations, and any visuals that you have collected that represent the life you want to create. This is a fun and creative way to manifest your deepest desires.

When you truly wake-up and become conscious of your life and what you are doing, that is when you can make some real changes. You can get therapy for your addiction(s), but the bottom line is **you need to want to change** your habits and your life. Sometimes we prefer to stay in our "shit" life because it's what we have become accustomed to, and often it's a life that we think we deserve.

It is also far easier to stay in what we know and in our comfort zones. It's easier to not even think too much about our lives as it's far too bloody painful. I believe one of the solutions is that once you **tap into your absolute amazingness and magnificence you will start to live the life that you deserve.**

"Are you ready to change your habits and your life so that your life is far more blissful?"

If like me, you are or were living a lie to yourself, this is not leading a great life. Start thinking about what will make a great life and then make a plan to create it. If you want to be able to create more stability and more bliss in your life, it will mean making some big changes and getting really honest about your current situation.

From a financial point of view, if you have been gambling excessively you could have experienced some huge gains and some huge losses. Consequently, you would go from having a huge amount of cash to some days having very little. This in itself creates instability and can cause a lot of stress and sleepless nights. It's like your life is just one giant roller-coaster, experiencing such high highs and then such low lows.

With gambling, like any addiction, I am not sure whether you are ever cured completely. It's something that can remain dormant and if you get really stressed and don't have some other coping mechanisms for reducing your stress, you can easily resort to gambling once again (or some other form of addiction). If succumbing to your addictions, the stress release will most likely only be a temporary feeling, and will most likely create even more imbalance in your life.

Do More of What You Love

One of the things that can help you during your recovery is to fill up your life with the things that you love and things that set your heart on fire. Find the things in your life that you are passionate about and make a conscious effort to do more of them. I also surround myself with inspirational and positive people, and really limit myself around people that are draining and/or negative.

Eventually significant changes were going to be made in my life when I began filling it up with things that I loved, and this really made a huge difference to my overall happiness. For example, as soon as I began writing once again, I remembered how much I loved it, and I actually started to think that I would rather be home writing than gambling! This was such a massive improvement and dramatic mindset change. Often you can replace one addiction with a much healthier one, as in my example, where writing became my new healthy "addiction".

In addition, I formed communities with like-minded women that were inspiring and supportive and brought extra joy to my life.

I felt a deep sense of connection that I had been missing all of my life. When I was gambling, I mostly did it alone. For years, it became something I did in solitude. It was no longer sociable and it was actually largely anti-sociable, to the point I would prefer not to speak to anyone, and would get annoyed if someone wanted to talk to me, especially guys. I was not there to pick anyone up; I was there to gamble.

Learning to love and honour myself more each day, made me realise that gambling, or any addictions were in fact the opposite of honouring me as a person, my time and my energy. As I learned to LOVE and honour myself more each day, the addictions eventually lessened dramatically, occasionally I would lapse back into that world, although there were many months of not having the desire to gamble at all. This was a HUGE improvement.

Although please note that I had a long-way to go before I would eventually take all of these key-lessons and utilise them. It was going to be a long-path before my gambling addictions were under control!

Value Your Life and Your Time

I learned to value my life, and how I spent my time, and whom I spent time with. My life became so much more joyful and peaceful, and I found that I didn't want to waste my time gambling. I slowly but surely began the process of choosing to do activities that were far more enjoyable and positive. I wanted to be around energy that was uplifting— not what you would usually find at a Casino or a Club, where the energy is mostly a very low vibration.

Stop Being so Hard on Yourself

If you have been gambling excessively, or have had some other addiction that has greatly affected your life, you need to learn to give yourself some slack and stop beating yourself up. If you do not stop the negative self-talk and beliefs, you may find that your addiction becomes even worse because of your low self-worth.

You also need to learn to forgive yourself, as this will hugely assist with your recovery. **You can change the present and the future, so please don't dwell on the past, as that cannot be changed.** You can learn from your mistakes and when you start valuing who you are, can then stop repeating your mistakes and toxic behaviour patterns. You are capable of creating a happier, peaceful, and more blissful life.

We all have choices, and if we continue down the "slippery slope" of addictions and leading an unconscious life, we can keep ourselves imprisoned in a horrid cycle of destructive and negative behaviour. If you remain in this state, you certainly cannot create a "deliciously divine" life that you are worthy of. Also, you will not be able to **tap into your genius zones.** You can very easily lose your sparkle and you could end up wasting all those wonderful gifts that you were born to utilise.

What is it that is still causing your suffering? Once you are aware of the cause then you can start to heal at a deeper level. You do not deserve to live a life of suffering, and you need to start believing you deserve so much more. ***We need to acknowledge that we have pain, not numb it out. We need to realise that this suffering is holding us back and we need to be courageous enough to ask for "permission" from ourselves to change and evolve.***

If we do not allow conscious change and healing, our lives can quickly become an absolute shipwreck. My life certainly did, and I do not want you to experience anything like that. If your life is currently a "shipwreck", get the help you need and make the changes that are required so that you can move forward and live a wonderful life. Be brutally honest with yourself and stop being blindsided.

Becoming Real About Your Problem

If you do have an addiction, it is very easy to ignore the fact that you have one. If you are or were anything like me, I would be in total denial for many years, not admitting to anyone that I had a gambling problem and going through the motions but wondering why my life was not as blissful as it could have been.

I continued on a destructive path of not dealing with my pain and not dealing with my past. Deciding to block it out, rather than deal with it, seemed easier. Do not be too proud or too stubborn and think everything is okay when it is actually NOT.

If you are suffering and numbing out with addictions and in denial of your life, you are just going through the motions of living a mediocre life. You are worthy of taking charge of your life and making the necessary changes. This may include getting some therapy if you are suffering, especially if your life is rapidly becoming out of control with your addictions.

The Power of Gratitude

I feel as part of your recovery, it is so vitally important that you still continue to utilise daily gratitude practices. **My belief is that when we concentrate on the good, the universe provides us with more "goodness", concentrate on the "bad" and the universe provides us with more "badness", as that's what we are expecting.**

Key Lessons:

- ❖ Go back to the fundamentals of personal development, utilising gratitude, visualisations and affirmations on a daily basis.
- ❖ Work on your self-love every day by honouring you and your time and where you place your energy and only accept things that are for your highest purpose.

- Create strong healthy boundaries.
- Ask for guidance from your guardian angels, soul tribe or spiritual guides.
- Utilise self-care practices daily.
- Do things that make your heart sing.
- Remove yourself from toxic situations and limit yourself around negative people.
- Set goals and create a plan for your life.
- Have some fun, for example go dancing, see a comedy, laugh more.
- Don't just live for the moment – think about your future.
- Really sit back and analyse your life and stop just going through the motions.
- Tap into your creativity again (this honestly saved me from a lifetime of gambling abuse).
- Join communities of women / attend women's retreats.
- Plan your next holiday.
- Study or refresh your mind with personal development teachings.
- Attend workshops / events that are motivational and inspiring.

"Happiness is when what you think, what you say, and what you do are in harmony"

– Mahatma Gandhi

Lesson 12

You are Worthy of Harmony

Meeting an Angel

It wasn't long before my lifeboat did arrive as I met a lovely older man who would become my next partner. After a few months of dating, he asked my daughter and I to live with him. I was reluctant at first, as I think I was still in recovery mode, extremely vulnerable, and still searching for someone else to rescue me.

After my initial reluctance, I finally accepted this delightful, caring man's offer (who seemed like an angel in disguise) and we became a new "family". He was such a decent man and he was intent on looking after me and my seven year old daughter. He even built a cubby house for her and he lovingly treated her like his own child.

This "angel" did actually fall in love with me and was so devoted and loving toward me. I also believe we were both extremely lonely when we met, and both craving a permanent committed relationship. We were very supportive and loving toward one another and became the best of friends.

One of the great advantages of moving to the suburbs, was that the local primary school turned out to be amazing and actually far better than the one my daughter had attended for the first two years. She very quickly settled into her new school, making new friends and loving it.

At this time in my life the physical strain was starting to show. I suffered extreme headaches and fatigue, and I would spend hours sleeping while my daughter was at school. When I wasn't working, or sleeping during the day, I was still struggling with my gambling addiction, which had escalated after the last abusive relationship. Unfortunately, this "angel" probably witnessed one of the hardest periods in my life, and there were many occasions where he didn't really experience the best side of me.

To help escape the emptiness I was feeling, I had joined a network marketing company (prior to meeting this man). Once we moved into together, we started running the business as a couple and, with his support, my business became far more successful by building a team of consultants.

I also got to experience fabulous overseas and interstate conferences, where I met some great women. One of these women I met all those years ago is still one of my friends today, and she is a complete blessing in my life. Many wonderful experiences were had from being part of this business, and it helped me to heal on various levels.

After a comfortable three years of living together, it was obvious that this man still adored me, however the relationship sadly became "just great friends". I began to feel that I was not attracted to him in the way a woman should be, and because of the way I was feeling, the intimacy had ceased.

I decided to leave this relationship and start another new journey. It was a courageous move, as I was living a very comfortable life. The problem was it didn't feel right, and he wasn't the man that I wanted an intimate relationship with. I also felt we didn't have a lot in common and decided I was too young at this time in my life, to not have that sexual chemistry with my man.

So once again I packed up our belongings, and even though there was a lot of angst felt and I also felt so very sad for M#3 who truly loved me, I did think at the time it was scary to be single again, but overall I thought it was a positive move. I knew that M#3 and I would always be friends and I did leave amicably. I found a lovely unit which was located not too far away. I wanted to stay in the area so my daughter could remain at her current primary school, as she was very happy there, and I didn't want to disrupt her life any more than I already had.

Whilst reviewing my manuscript, prior to printing, I sadly found out that this "Angel" had in actual fact become a real Angel in heaven as he passed away suddenly in August 2019. May you RIP beautiful man and thank you for your love and care and everything that you did for me.

Single motherhood was upon me again and I wasn't really interested in dating. However, my new neighbour insisted I meet one of her male friends who was single and she thought we would be compatible. She was extremely persistent and proceeded to organise a blind date with this Eastern European man.

On our first date, we met at the Crown Casino, which was not surprising as it became very apparent that he was a big gambler. (That should have been a red flag!) He seemed very pleasant and, admittedly, there was some mutual physical attraction between us. From that night onwards, we started to regularly date each other.

During our dating, we did share some good times together, in particular with our respective children and we were a great "family unit". My daughter was approximately nine, his daughter eleven and his son was seven. He developed a great relationship with my daughter, as I also did with his children. I absolutely adored them both. His children really did seem to love me and they would often say to me "you make our father a much nicer person and you bring out his best side". Their appreciation was very lovely and warmed my heart.

I was becoming wiser, as I refused to move in with him, and was determined to live separately. We slept over at each other's homes, particularly on weekends and school holidays, and we spent a lot of time together as a family. The family unit was a huge draw for me and, in many ways, towards the end of this relationship when I knew that the relationship was not good for me, I kept going back and he knew very clearly that he could manipulate me through the children.

Thank goodness I retained my independence and I had my own home, because if not, he would have tried to control me even more than he did as that is a common pattern of abusive people. Unfortunately, I ended up staying in this relationship for over seven years (although we did have two break-ups during this time). It would soon become obvious that I had in fact attracted my third abusive relationship, as he began to constantly verbally abuse me.

After the first break-up I formed a relationship with another man. We had a few months together and overall, he treated me very well, and he was a unique man who was probably one of the most sexually liberated men I had ever met. However, it wasn't long before I was back with my European gambling boyfriend, as I felt weak to his charms and missed his children as much as my daughter did.

Connecting to My Warrior Goddess Within

Unfortunately, the next time I left him, he threatened me with his criminal connections and stalked me. Regardless of his threatening behaviour, I ultimately decided to ignore his threats, connect with my inner-warrior woman and leave him once and for all. This was a very difficult thing to do, and I must admit, I had to dig deep once again and connect to huge courage within.

It's difficult to put into words, although it was like something just clicked within me and I finally made a very direct agreement with myself that I deserved a much better relationship. I remember making the decision that toxic and abusive relationships were no longer ever allowed into my life.

Breaking away from a controlling abusive relationship takes a lot of guts, determination and a huge amount of courage. It's not until you have gone through an abusive relationship yourself that you realise how difficult it can be to leave.

For me, the fear of being threatened, dealing with confused emotions, and the feeling of being so stuck, alone and damn right scared, had become very real. Fear can paralyse us and prevent us from leaving an abusive relationship, and it can seem impossible to leave. It's still surprising to some people, that you can be a strong, independent woman, and still fall prey to a toxic controlling relationship.

I started to think: what on earth is wrong with me? I would leave the good ones easily and then it would take me a long time to leave the abusive and toxic ones. Sustaining a relationship of any kind became a challenge for me to the point where I was wondering if I was even relationship material. I started to think that maybe I was destined to be on my own for the rest of my life. A part of me thought I would be better off never having another serious relationship. It all just seemed so challenging and painful.

Big Changes were Required

It was now obvious that I lacked so much self-worth and allowed myself to associate with guys that were not in alignment with my highest purpose. To break this cycle, I once again started utilising affirmations, visualisations, and further self-worth practices that I had learnt many years ago.

I also invested in many clearings and healings and worked vigorously on my personal development once again. The conscious part of me knew that I needed to make a lot of changes, and I was also now prepared to admit a lot of my mistakes in order to start to make wiser life choices.

Building my Self-Worth

Time after time I had kept sabotaging my happiness and putting up with crappy relationships. I was now starting to build on my self-worth, yet again, and started to realise that I did deserve a better relationship, but I needed to start with the relationship I had with myself, first.

I needed to honour and respect *me* first and foremost, before I could attract a healthy loving relationship. Finally, I realised that it was far healthier to **not** be in a relationship than to put up with a mediocre, or even worse, an abusive relationship. **This was a huge paradigm shift for me and I believe this is when the real changes started to occur.**

Visualising a Loving and Respectful Relationship

Deep down in my heart, I really did want a serious relationship and it was only my stupid fears that made me think I didn't want to commit to another one. I knew that I had to start visualising and affirming the exact life and relationship that I wanted to create.

Finally, I started to believe I was worthy of a decent loving genuine relationship and I had to dig deep for extra courage to pursue one. I felt there was still hope and decided I wasn't going to give up on the possibility of falling in love again and creating a wonderful life with someone else.

> ***"As long as there is life, there is hope"* - Bryant McGill**

Your Path to Creating Harmony

I hope that your life is very harmonious and will continue down the path of peace and tranquillity, because this is what you deserve. However, if you feel that harmony in your life has been missing, I have listed some of my key recommendations that can help you on your path of living harmoniously and attracting a relationship that is loving, respectful, and fills you with joy.

Learning your Lessons

Make sure you recover and heal from any previous relationships prior to starting a new one, allowing yourself time to stop and breathe and think about what you really want. Don't ignore all of your personal development knowledge and go back to the fundamentals, if your life is not where you want it to be.

I don't think that we attract abusive relationships because we are bad people but, perhaps on some level, we do think that we are deserving of bad relationships. When you love and honour yourself, you will **not** attract the toxic relationship in the first place, and this will allow you to break the pattern of attracting controlling and abusive relationships.

Energetically, I also think that we can often attract the wrong type of relationship when we do not feel worthy. We need to learn to protect our own energies, particularly if we are sensitive, otherwise we are too open and can attract lower vibrations. **You need to stop thinking that someone is going to save you, as you are the only person who can save yourself.**

When you fall in love with you, first and foremost, it is much more likely that you will attract a more loving, respectful and wonderful relationship.

Connect to Your Courage

Breaking away from a controlling abusive relationship is not easy, and anyone who has experienced this will understand how difficult it can be. Not only does it take much courage, but also a willingness to understand that you actually do deserve better. You also need to realise that you will survive when you do leave.

Fear is a huge factor that keeps people in abusive relationships. That's the irony; you are fearful when you are in the relationship, and also fearful about leaving it. You need to keep convincing yourself that you will be much happier when you do actually leave.

Once you leave, know that you can rebuild your life and that you will **never** have to put up with abusive relationships ever again. You can live in peace and harmony, and with no need to live your life in fear and regret, feeling worthless and controlled. You can start to heal, love yourself more, and day by day, you will become stronger and know that you've made the right choice.

You deserve so much more, and you need to decide that under no circumstances will you accept being treated badly, abused or controlled. As soon as you make that decision, you can rebuild your confidence and your life can then change. You need to get to a stage where you'll say "I am done! I am done with being treated unlovingly, I am done with not honouring myself, I am done with attracting abusive relationships."

Know that you can rebuild your life, you can learn to be strong once again and you can reprogram your mind to NOT attract controlling abusive relationships.

Slowly but surely you can rebuild your life, and even though it may be challenging at times, it will be worth it to get your life back on track. You will look back and be proud of what you've done and how you had the courage to leave. At the same time, visualise the exact life that you do want, and keep that vision alive every single day to bring your vision into reality.

Financial Control

In abusive relationships, there can often be a clear pattern of financial control and often the woman is financially dependent on the man. Or she may have been financially independent prior to or at the start of the relationship, but slowly the abusive partner will start to take control.

When you continue to build your self-worth and self-esteem and keep believing in yourself and your abilities, then financial control is less likely to happen. I think that it is wise to have some financial independence, no matter what your circumstances are, as this will help you to feel much more empowered.

If you do decide to leave an abusive relationship, and don't have your own income at that time, you can still actively look for work and/or build your own business at your pace. Your safety and peace of mind is far more important. Luckily for Australians, we have many government assistance programs to help you financially until you establish yourself.

You may not get your dream job to start with or be making a fortune in your business, but you will be much happier. Some initial sacrifices with your lifestyle will be well worth it when you have your serenity once again. The sense of peace that you'll feel when you do not have to worry about being abused, ridiculed, manipulated, judged or controlled each day will make it all worth it.

Initially, it can be very scary to leave, as you may have become accustomed to a certain lifestyle and in a "comfort zone". It can be a huge relief having the bills paid by someone else, going out to expensive restaurants and on exclusive holidays. But remember, you deserve a peaceful and safe home, not one where you are "living on the edge", being controlled and feeling powerless and worthless.

As you start to build your own financial independence, you will never have to feel financially controlled again. You need to believe in yourself and start to manifest your desires.

Not All Men are Bastards

Not all men are bastards. There are some lovely men out there so don't be a "man basher" by putting them all in one category and becoming bitter and twisted. Many men have also been abused in one way or another, or have had to deal with loss, betrayal and grief. These feelings are not gender based, and you cannot take your pain out on someone who does not deserve it. It's important that we are able to release our past suffering and realise how many amazing people are out there.

Once you begin the process of building your own self-worth is when you will start to attract a different type of relationship that is far healthier. However, **you must work on yourself first and foremost, including healing, forgiveness and mindset adjustments prior to getting into yet another relationship.** Take your time, invest in you and stop worrying about having a relationship and take the time to get to know *you* and fall in love with *you*.

Imagine if I hadn't had the courage to leave the last toxic and abusive relationship. I would have continued leading a very mediocre life with maybe some moments of happiness, particularly with the children; however, I would be wondering why these were only temporary. If I didn't leave or didn't change, I would not have met my future husband. I would not be feeling enormous gratitude, love and happiness that comes with mutual love and respect. I certainly would not have planned an incredible wedding to my future Mr. Worthy. My life would be exceptionally different in all ways.

We all have choices and none of us need to lead a mediocre life. **If your life is not where you want it to be, make the changes that are needed and dig deep into your courage and connect with that warrior goddess in you to support and guide you**.

Don't waste another day in a second-rate relationship that is abusive and toxic where you are not respected, loved and honoured. If you are being abused in any way, shape, or form, you can create a plan to leave and rebuild your life again. You are stronger than you think and you will be amazed how your life will begin to change when you make the change. **It's like the universe has been waiting for you to say "enough is enough, I deserve better"**.

All of your supporters who love and care for you will be relieved, as they also know that you deserve much better. You also need to start believing this and start planning a wonderful future. Draw on every part of your strength and absolutely know that without a doubt, you are worth a harmonious and fabulous life.

Key Lessons:

Don't make the mistake of thinking the following:

- You are not good enough to attract any better- we all deserve a loving and amazing relationship with ourselves and with others.

- Things will get better – he will change / I will help change him. At times, you will have better days/nights, however it's unlikely that it will last and you will again be at the mercy of this controlling toxic relationship. You are the one to change, as the other person will only change if they have deep healing and are accountable for their own actions.

- **How will I survive financially**? This is a very common fear and one that often keeps you in a bad relationship. Know that you can get a job and start earning your own income – you can start afresh. Know that you do not have to rely on your partner financially anymore – you need to connect to your courage and know that you can be totally independent in this area of your life.

- Seek a professional to help you, as it's not an easy journey and extra support and guidance is well recommended.

"You cannot be healed while you hold on to pain, you must let it go, so that your heart is free to embrace love again"

– Leon Brown

Lesson 13

You Are Worthy of Finding Love Again

Throughout my life, I have experienced so much grief, loss and betrayal when it came to many of the relationships I attracted. In fact, many would describe my life as being like a "soap-opera", however this was no movie or television script!

I certainly had my reservations about finding true love again after everything I had experienced. You could imagine, after my traumatic circumstances, that I would have huge concerns about ever forming a serious relationship and would be reluctant to ever trust a man enough to want to get married for a second time.

Some of the questions I started to ask myself as I was becoming more consciously aware were:

- ❖ *Why was I on this path of victimhood?*
- ❖ *Why was I on this path of self-destruction and self-abuse?*
- ❖ *Why did I think I was not worthy of true love and commitment?*

To say that I was quite scarred and a lot of heart healing was required would be an understatement. Surprisingly though, even after my experiences, I still never gave up hope and somehow kept my faith and intuitively felt that I would fall in love again. I did feel that eventually I could learn to trust myself and in turn trust another man. There deep within my tortured heart lay a glimmer of hope that I could completely heal and learn to trust once again.

My trust had clearly been betrayed many times throughout my life; however, I still remained optimistic I could attract that special person. I wasn't going to give up on love or the hope that I could find someone I could fully commit to and love once again. I suspected that it would be a big journey, but one I needed to take if I wanted to attract a life partner.

Clearly, I have shown that I have had numerous relationships over the years. Although some were very toxic and abusive, there were also some that were with decent and loving men who were not all bad. Now I can clearly see that I had developed a pattern in my life. I had, in actual fact, become a "serial relationship rejecter".

I eventually left most of the relationships I formed. Some were terrible and abusive, and of course I should have left those particular ones, and have no doubt this was the right decision in those circumstances. However, some of my relationships were with decent loving and caring men and I would leave those ones as well. I thought maybe I was just "not a relationship type of girl" and that maybe I was destined to be on my own.

It was 2008 that my life would change forever and it was at this point that I had said to myself *"What are you doing with your life? Don't you think enough is enough of abusive and toxic relationships? Don't you think you are worth committing yourself to another man?"*

At this time. I was 44 years old and working hard to provide a great lifestyle for both myself and my 15-year old daughter. I had done considerable work on my personal development, but the journey is never really complete, and there are always different layers and new lessons to learn.

What I started to feel was a lot more clarity on what I did want in my life and I was done with toxic or abusive relationships. It was at this point that I began to visualise and affirm a true love connection with my future life partner.

Meeting my Husband-to-Be

Of course, there are no coincidences; however, through a chance meeting at a café in Bayside Melbourne, I recognised an ex-colleague from many years ago. He didn't recognise me at first, as I was about 20 kilos heavier, and I had dyed my hair blonde.

I decided to go out of my comfort zone and went straight over to him and introduced myself, I said that I recognised him but was unsure from where. It then became evident that we had met all those years ago when we both worked in the banking industry at the same office in Collins St, Melbourne.

We hadn't known each other that well while working together, and it was only the occasional meeting in the lift that we would greet each other with a nod and a smile. At this time, in the late 80's/early 90s, he was married and had just started a family, and I had just met my first husband to be and was happy and madly in love. We did not have any romantic connection at all, but interestingly enough, I recognised his face from all those years ago.

This was to become one fated "accidental" coffee meeting as there was no way in the world that I consciously knew I was going to be meeting up with my future second husband that very morning! After I boldly approached him, we got chatting, exchanged some of our life experiences over all those years, spoke about our children, laughed, and truly connected at that destined meeting.

Our connection was very strong from that moment and it was difficult to ignore. Believe me, I had been fooled before, so I had to really think about it and feel into my intuition whether this was real or not. That was the beginning of a beautiful courtship and I knew instantly that this relationship was going to be very different from all the others. This was a man that I felt so comfortable with and felt I this inner knowing that we would eventually fall in love.

He seemed so familiar to me, like I had known him for many years, even lifetimes. It was pure destiny and divine timing as there was no other way to describe this "coincidental" meeting. I even tried to fight these feelings and convince myself I was wrong.

I wasn't wrong, and my intuition was spot on. We did fall in love and this man would eventually become my second husband, my Mr. Worthy! From this day forward, my life completely changed forever, and this relationship has become one of my greatest love stories.

After dating for a few months, my new love received a great work opportunity, and he decided he would relocate to Canberra in 2008 with his eldest son. We then began a long-distance relationship, as at the time I remained in our home town, Melbourne with my daughter. My new love also had a middle son who was living in Melbourne as well with his mother.

Admittedly, I was a Melbourne girl, and didn't have any inclination to move. My daughter and I were living in an amazing apartment, which was extremely comfortable and one that I truly adored. Not only that, I also had my daughter to think about, her schooling and also the fact that she had a boyfriend in Melbourne.

The benefit of this type of arrangement was that it also gave us both some breathing space for reflection and contemplation of our relationship. It became very apparent that we missed each other immensely; however, it would take another six months for him to convince us to leave our beloved home town!

Before I could contemplate the big move and change my daughters and my life completely, I firstly had to know that I truly loved and could commit fully to this man. I also had to know that he truly loved me and the feelings were completely mutual. I was over the superficial bullshit relationships and wasn't going to make the move if there was not mutual true love shared. Once I realised that I actually did love this man and he loved me, I intuitively knew that to move interstate was the right decision to make. Something had truly shifted in my heart and it was just a deep knowing.

Looking back, it was still risky and I was very naive when it came to the challenges of the blended family dynamics. However, if it didn't work out I would either start a new life in Canberra or return to Melbourne. The best thing that could happen is that we would begin the start of a loving committed relationship and build a life together.

I was never afraid of taking risks throughout my life, however this time was so much more centred, and I was connecting to my intuition as well. I felt something different, deep within my heart, and my inner-wisdom was telling me that all would be okay and it was the right thing to do. At long last, I was finally waking up and becoming more conscious, and I was also starting to really trust my intuition. My question at this point in my life was "Am I now truly becoming Love Worthy?"

Your Path to Finding Love Again

Please do not live a life of doubt and fear and allow yourself to unlock the door to love. Make a choice **to heal, grow, and start believing in love once again**. You can either make a lot of excuses or you can choose to open the door to the possibility of love.

My recommendation for you, if you are really wanting to bring a love relationship into your life, is that you:

Unlock and then open the door to the possibility of love regardless of your past suffering

I think one of the biggest traps that many women fall into is that they are not even open to the possibility of finding love again. Instead, choosing to close the door and locking it securely, as their heart was so hurt and damaged that they feel it was easier to do this, than the possibility of heartbreak once again.

I have witnessed many women locking out the feelings, locking out any attempt to even attract the right person and locking out even the possibility of love and commitment with a life partner. It saddens me as they are giving up on the possibility of meeting a love partner and in turn, energetically never attracting, but repelling a potentially wonderful life partner.

It does take courage to move forward and it involves a certain level of risk. That "risk" could be worth it when you open yourself up to the possibility of what could be a life changing and amazing relationship.

We All have Choices

We all have a choice to either run and hide or we can open ourselves up to living a more meaningful and loving life with another person. I personally don't think most of us are geared towards being alone for the rest of our days, not sharing our dreams, adventures or intimacy with anyone else.

We need to take the time to pause and think about what we really want and know deep within our hearts and souls what truly makes us happy. We really need to make the choice to heal from our suffering and to open our hearts once again. I have found that many just want to keep the door shut and not even attempt to open it.

You need to stop putting up with an unhealthy relationship or going from one relationship to another with the fear of committing and sabotaging any chance of future happiness. Don't shut yourself off completely from the possibility of finding another big love!

You Do Not have to be Lonely

Are you open to the possibility of bringing a real love relationship back into your life? Are you ready to release your fears from previous failed relationships, or if fear has such a strong hold on you, can you feel the fear and just do it regardless?

Feel the fear and just do it regardless

If you answered YES to the above, you can then start to bring this into your energy, into your world and into your heart. You do not have to continue to suffer and you do not have to continue to be lonely and disconnected from the possibility of love. Of course, you want to be able to **love you first and you want to love your own company, heal from your past suffering and then start to unlock and then open your own door to the possibility of love.**

Becoming Conscious

It's time for you to become completely conscious of your life, learning from your mistakes and allowing yourself to feel rather than "numbing out". Once you are able to do this, you can then create a clear vision of what you actually do want to attract, accompanied with a plan to move forward, and then implement this plan.

Unfortunately, your life will not be improved when you are not being real about your life and numbing out your pain. You will block the possibility of finding true love once again. You may even be starting to feel exhausted in your search for love or lack of love, and may even be feeling very complacent about the whole "love" concept.

I really hope that you do not give up on the possibility of finding love once again and you don't think it's all too hard. If you want to live a life without a partner, of course, that's your choice. However, if you are over being on your own, then start to get real about your life, and do the healing and the work that is required. Start to trust the flow of the universe, trust your heart, and trust your intuition.

Changing the Victim Mentality

Are you hanging onto that old dialogue and that old record of being a victim? If you are, replace your thoughts with such things as "I am no longer a victim of my circumstances, I am now ready to make the required changes, including changing the way I think about relationships and the lies that I continually tell myself and others".

Your new mantra could become:

I am ready to heal, move on, and open my heart once again

It's now time for you to **wake-up and it is time for you to do some more personal development, invest in your healing, and start to make conscious choices**. It may also be time for you to go back to some key fundamentals to improve your own life.

Stop the Self-Sabotage

I think subconsciously we often self-sabotage our lives. Personally, I kept deviating from my true purpose and taking the difficult path, sabotaging my happiness, and not tuning in to what could be potentially a much happier existence.

Do not **be your own worst enemy thinking that you only deserve an average life. Then you will be far less likely to not keep choosing the difficult path**. Start thinking more broadly and make bigger expectations for yourself. This includes demanding more happiness, more LOVE, more abundance and more passion and knowing that you were not born to live a mediocre life, but a magnificent one.

You also need to ban the negative self-talk and replace with positive thoughts and you need to stop telling yourself those lies about yourself. You need to ban the "mean" girl. Reprogram your mind and start saying how wonderful you are, loving "YOU" and most importantly knowing how LOVE WORTHY you are!

You may not believe it at first, but you can trick your mind initially. Eventually, dynamically you will start to believe and that's when your life will change in so many ways for the better.

These are my key strategies that will help you to find love once again:

- ❖ Believe in YOU once again.
- ❖ Ban the negative self-talk and negative behavioural patterns.
- ❖ Stop being a victim and decide that you will not stay "stuck" in your pain and suffering and that you can move on.
- ❖ Know that you are more powerful than you think and you can make better choices for yourself.
- ❖ Know that your past does not define your future and that you can move on and create an amazing future.
- ❖ Know that you are the master of your destiny and you can make the necessary changes to make sure you are creating a magnificent life.

- ❖ Be completely accountable and do the work – no blaming, no excuses and truly believing your worth and how amazing you truly are.
- ❖ Be proud, be courageous and be determined in your search to become a better version of YOU.

Visualising and Setting Clear Intentions:

I believe in setting clear intentions, creating affirmations and visualisations can really assist in creating the life that you truly desire. Refusing to allow your inner torment and pain to prevent you from future happiness, certainly helps you to attract a new relationship.

Living in the Past Blocks your Future Happiness

I have also witnessed women who appear to have it all together; however, they are so lonely and they are longing for a relationship deep down in their heart and soul. The problem is that they are too scared to even try another relationship because they're still living in the past. They may have been so hurt, they decide they don't want to go through any more pain, so they don't even give love a chance.

When this occurs, I believe people are blocking themselves of ever finding a partner because of their past fears and suffering they are hanging onto. They also believe that everything else is working in their life, so they don't need or want a life partner. I think that this is just an excuse and an avoidance mechanism so that they can protect their wounded heart.

Wise questions to ask yourself:

- ❖ Have you stopped the search for a relationship because of your fears?

- Are you blocking your future happiness because you haven't completely healed, forgiven and moved on from your past suffering?
- Do you think all men are bastards and not worth the effort?
- Do you need to fall more in love with you, trust you and honour you, so that you can then attract that amazing and loving relationship?
- Are you looking for Mr. Perfect?
- Are you trying to be Ms. Perfect?

Every person deserves some form of companionship and intimacy. On the other hand, some people do not necessarily want to get married again or live with another person to have this form of intimacy, and that's a very personal choice.

I simply hope that you are not closing yourself off to the possibility of creating an amazing committed relationship on your own terms. My wish for you is that your fears and unresolved pain don't prevent you from future happiness. What that means to you will be a personal choice.

Key Lessons:

- Fall in love with "YOU" first and then you will attract a much more loving and respectful relationship.
- Do not be desperate and settle on any relationship because you are lonely.
- Don't shut yourself off from feeling once again - open your "door" and be open to the possibilities of falling in love once again.
- Take some risks and put your fears in the corner, or do it scared regardless.

- ❖ Start believing in yourself again, building your confidence and self-worth.
- ❖ Heal your heart, forgive your heart, open your heart.

"Friends are medicine for a wounded heart, and vitamins for a hopeful soul"

— Steve Maraboli

Lesson 14

You are Worthy of Friendship

As far as friendships were concerned, for many years I didn't really have many close female friends I could rely on. Unfortunately, just when I thought I could trust them, I would find that they were jealous and/or competitive with me. I loved my sister; however, she had a large group of friends and we didn't hang out that much together, so at times I felt disconnected from her as well.

Preferring the Company of Males – Healing the Past

In my early 20s, one of my closest friends was a male gay friend. I am sure if he wasn't gay I may very well have married him. We both studied theatre and drama together, became the best of mates and were compatible on so many levels. Our lovely dates would consist of going to restaurants and our favourite was going to the local theatres.

We also became members of the Melbourne Theatre company and we would frequent the Victorian Arts Centre, seeing some marvellous shows. I had quickly grown out of nightclubs, and anything to do with theatre and/or food was my preferred choice of entertainment, as I detested the cigarette smoke and was never a big drinker. I was lucky to find another single person who had the same interests we could share together.

Looking back on my life, I think that there were many periods where I actually preferred the company of males. My paradigm at the time was that females seemed to be either nasty, competitive or I merely didn't seem to connect with their energy. I felt excluded from many female groups and it was easier to avoid being attached to any form of group.

On the occasion when I was accepted into a group, I felt uncomfortable and not truly connected with anyone. I found that many women seemed to like me, but there was something within my energy that was keeping them at a distance and prevented establishing any real closeness. I struggled with finding a "bestie" type of friendship that was equal on both sides and I knew I had to become my own best friend.

At the same time, I longed for close female friendships, particularly as I got into my 40s. Here was another huge realisation that I was the one that needed to change if I was going to attract more loyal and loving friendships. I also had to clear that energy that women were mostly nasty, competitive or could not be trusted. It was no wonder that I was energetically keeping any potential close female friendships at a distance.

Unfortunately, many of my female friendships had turned out to be not what I thought they were, and I was fooling myself thinking that they were true friends who aligned with my friendship values. It took me a long time to realise that they were not. My values include having each other's back, not competing with each other, supporting one another during the good times and the bad, and being loyal and honest.

In my 20's I remember I had one girlfriend who joined me for drinks one evening, whilst I was also meeting the guy I was dating at the time. The entire evening, she flirted quite substantially with him, fluttering the eyelashes and giving those "suggestive" looks. The whole "flirty flavour" body language was projected and it was like she was constantly craving his attention to prove a point that she was far more desirable than me.

Upon returning home with my date and after being intimate together, he told me that during sex he could not stop thinking of my girlfriend! Needless to say, that relationship did not last much longer, and I never quite trusted that girlfriend again. Not to mention that at a deeper level it would have affected my self-worth and questioned the way that I looked and why wasn't I sexy enough for him to be fully into me! Wow that would be a big lesson to learn and realise that we are not going to be attractive to everyone but that doesn't mean we are not sexy and attractive. We have to start believing this ourselves!

Even though it could have been unconscious behaviour on her part, and she was indeed very insecure, I just felt hurt and flattened by this type of behaviour. I didn't have the wisdom, nor the self-worth I have now, to process exactly what was occurring and how to deal with it far more proactively.

Displaying Courage to have Honest Conversations

This was also a great example of where I needed to have the courage to have an honest conversation and tell my girlfriend that it was crossing our friendship boundary. In my mind, it was an unspoken friendship code of what we expect from our girlfriends, but I lacked the courage to voice this.

By all means be friendly to your friend's partner, but DO NOT openly flirt and parade around like someone who is desperate for attention and competing for more attention to prove your desirability. It's a low act and, in my opinion, it is not accepted within the "friendship code".

Changing my Vibration

Regardless of my previous disappointments and betrayals, I really began to have a deep desire to build longer lasting and deeper friendships and connections with other women. It was like something different was stirring within and I was starting to recognise that it was a part of my life that had been lacking for far too long.

It was also around this time when I knew I had to do some healing around the girls who bullied me at primary school, previous girlfriends who were untrustworthy and other not very reliable or loyal friends. In particular, the ones that had crossed my personal boundaries with no respect or understanding of the hurt that they caused. I knew that there were great women around, **I just needed to connect to them and change my vibration so I could attract a different type of energy**.

Real friendships were Formed

Changes were starting to occur and in 1999, after all that betrayal from my most intimate relationships and feeling so lost and disconnected, I did start to create some lovely female friendships. Some of the women were through my daughter's school and some were through a multi-level marketing company that I had joined. These friendships were an integral part of my healing and helped me to restore my faith in female friendships.

Because of this attitude, I met one of my favourite women in my life. We instantly connected and we even lived around the corner from each other, so we started to see a lot of each other in both our business and personal worlds. She also became like an "auntie" to my daughter, and her genuine love for people and her huge beautiful heart was so very refreshing and so appreciated.

To this day, this beautiful woman is still all heart, and I love that she is in my life. I love and adore her, and even though we do not see each other that much these days and we live in different states, nothing has changed between us. It's friendships like this that can literally change your life and also help heal you from past experiences that were not positive. I think this was the catalyst for me beginning to build strong female friendships.

Not so long after this time, I also formed a very close friendship with another amazing woman. She also lives interstate, and similarly whenever we see each other it's like it was yesterday. She is a woman who I trust with my life, who has never judged me, and as a real test to our friendship has lent me money at times (particularly in those single motherhood days).

She never hesitated during those times when I required a temporary loan, and this itself tells you a lot about someone. These women gave me hope that real genuine female friendships can exist in my world and I have continued to build other fabulous female friendships.

The "Goddess" Wedding Table

At my wedding, I had a "Goddess Table", and invited some of these women whom I loved, adored and appreciated. It was unfortunate I couldn't invite all women in my goddess communities, because it was a small, intimate wedding, however having selecting a few to attend at one of the most important events of my life; was extremely special to me.

I am never complacent with my friendships and I honour each and every one of these women. I also thank them so much for the lessons they have taught me, for the love and support they have shown me, and for helping me to find and tap into my own feminine beauty and essence as a woman.

Friendship Challenges

I feel very blessed I have been able to create some beautiful friendships with women that I trust, love and adore. There were times though when I felt challenged with some of my friendships, and wondered how loyal and committed these women were to me. I have a high regard for my friendships, and it's only in recent years I have realised that unless they support, love me and are loyal and committed as I am to them, then it's not worth the effort to allow them into my "inner sanctuary".

This was difficult for me at first and I would become so obsessed if I didn't feel the friendship was reciprocated. It was a painful lesson to realise many times I held them in much higher regard than they did me. It was a harsh truth, but one I had to acknowledge so I didn't keep investing in the friendship to the same extent.

I have now learned the art of setting clearer boundaries and being able to voice my truth in a direct but loving way. I still honour these women and wish them the very best, but am slowly learning the art of who I can include in my inner sanctuary, and who is worth my absolute loyalty and love.

Your Path to Creating Friendships

Female friendships should never be under-estimated and is one area of our lives that we need to make sure is continuing to thrive. I think that it's fabulous to have a partner and close family members, but having girlfriends is a very different dynamic. From my personal experiences, friendships can add another whole dimension of contentment to your life. Whether you are single, dating or in a committed relationship, it is worth working on your cherished friendships.

We need to make time for our friends and organise regular catch-ups, as it can be easy to get caught up with other aspects of our lives. It's important and extremely healthy to have your own independent friendships, outside of your partner. Enjoy a social life that is not totally revolved around your relationship. Nurture your friendships and make time for them. We need our "girly" nights (and even weekends away) as it will help nourish and awaken our mind, body, and soul.

As we get older, I think we become wiser and attract like-minded women and women that support, guide and love you. We can also really start to utilise our intuition, allowing ourselves to not accept the fake friendships as we become aware of who is genuine and who isn't. It's also wise to be more discriminating as to who we allow into our "inner sanctuary" and who we choose to spend our time with. Life is busy and short, so we need to work out who is really worth spending time with.

Setting Clear Friendship Boundaries

When you set a really clear intention and boundary on what sort of friendships you want to create and sustain, that is when healthier and happier friendships can be formed. As your vibration changes, some friendships will naturally dissolve, making the way for new friendships that are more aligned with you energetically.

In addition, to attract great friendships you also need to be a great friend. Loyalty and the unspoken friendship code is essential for a healthy and happy friendship and we should not accept anything less. You need to give, to listen, to guide and be supportive, and then you will also create friendships like that as well. A friendship is totally one-sided when you are the one constantly giving, it needs to be a friendship that is reciprocated. You both need to be around for each other in the good and the bad and even the ugly moments.

Be a Great Friend to Attract a Great Friend

Are your Friendship Values Aligned?

I feel conflicts arise with your friendships when your value systems are not aligned and you have different perspectives. This will usually occur very early within the friendship, as you are both getting to know each other. If one of your highest values is friendship, and one of your "friends" value system is quite different, then you need to realise that there may be some issues to contend with if the friendship continues.

Sometimes you decide to give 100 percent to the friendship, and if your new friend doesn't have the same friendship values, you'll need to have an honest discussion together. If you don't, you can run the risk of continuing to put so much into the friendship, that you will start to feel resentment, because you are not getting the same dedication back. It's so important to be able to openly communicate your feelings and tell your friend how you feel and if they have upset you for whatever reason, connect to your courage, and be open with them.

We should only give what we are comfortable giving, and not have an expectation that they will give as much back. Although in saying that, I also feel there needs to be a balance in your friendships. If you are constantly the one giving, then it's not very balanced and you'll need to reassess your friendship and whether it is working for you.

You don't need to hang onto friendships that are no longer serving you or are not for your highest purpose. Know that you do not need to settle when it comes to good quality friendships and that having one or a few close friends is worth far more than a dozen mediocre ones.

We all deserve friends who are loyal, trustworthy, and never cross that line if they value your friendship. Don't allow wounds from the past to affect your ability to form close friendships, and know that you can heal and learn to trust women again.

It's like any relationship - we need to know that we are worthy of great friendships, that we can be accepted as we are, we can voice our truth without damaging the friendship and we can connect to our courage so we can openly express our boundaries, even at the risk sometimes of damaging our friendship.

When we are fragile or suffer from low self-worth, we can often keep our thoughts and feelings to ourselves wanting desperately to keep the friendship alive. This is the wrong vibration as we will then wonder why we feel so unhappy about the friendship and wonder why it's not as healthy as it could be if there was open loving communication.

If you have formed a genuine friendship, it will survive and you will become even stronger, knowing that you are safe to speak your truth. Like any relationship, it's better to not have the friendship if it's a toxic one and is constantly draining you. Take a stand that you will only attract wonderful loyal friends who enrich your life, and then your path to creating friendships will be a much smoother and enjoyable one.

Do not settle for the friendships that bring you no joy, where you cannot speak your truth and there is no mutual support and respect.

I highly recommend that you go out and meet other like-minded women with a very clear intention of what you are searching for. It may be far more powerful and life-changing than what you ever thought possible.

Key Lessons:

- Never underestimate how much joy a friendship can provide you.
- Make the time for your friendships and don't devote all your time to your partner/children/business.
- Heal from your past wounds when it comes to female friendships.
- Know what your friendship values are and what your boundaries are and do not be afraid to voice these in a loving and direct way.
- Do not accept mediocre and toxic friendship with "emotional vampires" who drain you.
- Be discriminating with the types of friends you choose and only allow genuine, supportive and loving friends into your "inner sanctuary". Not everyone is going to be your "bestie". Do not be obsessed about friendships and want to feel like someone's "bestie".
- You need to be your own best friend and the right people will then be part of your life. You need to love and accept yourself first and foremost.

"*Alone we can do so little; together we can do so much*"

– Helen Keller

Lesson 15

You are Worthy of Community

Craving a Community

Creating and being part of a community seemed to be quite elusive until I got into my late 40s. I felt a deep sense of loss around not being part of communities of women in the past. I consciously decided that I wanted to attract not only cherished friendships but a community of women. A "tribe" of women that I could feel connected to, where there was no judgement, no competition, only a beautiful collective of women honouring and supporting each other.

I wanted to be part of communities of women where we all celebrated each other's successes and where we did not compete or compare. A gathering of women that would create so much "magic" and an energy that would be healing and empowering. I knew in my heart that these communities did exist.

It wasn't long after this intention, when I actually started to become involved with women's events, workshops, and circles. It was at this time I also realised that being part of these communities of women would fill one of the missing parts of the "happiness puzzle" of my life. Joining women's circles would also be the major catalyst for healing my wounds around female friendships and feeling connected once again.

In 2013, I attended the "You Can Do It" Hay House Seminar at the Melbourne Convention Centre. There were big inspirational names present such as Deepak Chopra, Wayne Dyer, Doreen Virtue and Sonia Choquette. Unfortunately, one of my biggest influences, Louise Hay was not present, but regardless, it was a remarkable event and full of so many other inspirational leaders.

It was a truly incredible two days, and afterwards, I felt some shifts in my heart and my soul stirring. I believe I was sending out unconscious messages to the universe looking for more in my life. That saying "when the student is ready, the teacher will appear" was about to be very true in my life.

Attending a Life-Changing Event

I began adopting a habit of setting intentions for each year and also choosing a word for the year to help me keep on track and stay focussed. At the start of 2014, I remember my chosen words for the year were "friendship" and "community". I was also still searching for closer connections and I craved some form of deeper connection with women, while being open to receiving guidance from the universe.

My now husband (partner at the time), knew how I was feeling and what my intentions were, and he genuinely wanted to help me. It was around March 2014 that he discovered an event that he thought I would be interested in attending and may be able to help with my quest. This event was hosted by Luanne Mareen.

I didn't know Luanne at this stage or any of the women in her community. What I did know however, was that I completely trusted my intuition and knew I needed to be at this three-day event, even without knowing a single soul attending it. I booked with an inner knowing that I needed to just go. As it turned out, that decision was going to be life-changing in the most fabulous way, and would start me on a whole new exciting journey of community and friendship.

I attended the event with an open mind and an open heart, and it turned out to be everything I wanted and needed and so much more than I anticipated. This event stirred something deep within and it completely awakened my feminine energy. I not only connected to a wonderful community of women at the event, I also continued to develop many life changing friendships. These communities of women continue to this day to be a source of love, support and shared wisdom.

This is a great example where clear intentions and even choosing a word for the year can be so very powerful. At the start of 2014, I had so much clarity around wanting to create new female friendships, and being a part of amazing communities. My words "friendship" and "community" were really starting to manifest in obvious ways.

I had set powerful intentions to be part of strong amazing communities and without any coincidence, I was then going to an event full of over 100 women that would change my life in profound ways. I really believe when you are very clear on your intentions and you have your words for the year, the universe will conspire with you to make it happen.

The Importance of Community

The realisation of the importance of community became so clear to me, and it was then that I found part of the puzzle that had been missing in my life. It's even hard to put into words how much more happiness and peace I felt on a deep level.

All of the distrust and disconnection was replaced by complete love, support and connection with a community of amazing women. My faith and trust with regard to forming communities of women had been restored, and for the first time in my life, I felt a deep sense of belonging and connection.

Birthing my New Business

Whilst I was at this event, I also signed up for a high-end coaching program for 12 months where I was inspired to birth my new business, which I initially named "Worthy Goddess".

I was also going to learn that running a business is certainly not for the faint-hearted, as it will reveal not only your strengths, but all of your weaknesses, in very obvious ways. I learned that running a business would take endless amounts of stamina, courage, resilience and the need to believe in myself like I have never done before. I also now realise that you need to ask the right questions to get the most from your coaching program, which is challenging when you are a new starter.

I was on a mission to learn more and expand my knowledge so I attended many courses within a 2-year time frame. I knew I also had a deep calling to bring communities of women together and began facilitating my own *"Magnificent You"* goddess gatherings. I also began attending other women's circles, events, workshops and retreats on a regular basis and I felt connected to so many wonderful communities of women.

The Worthy Goddess Community

I have created a Facebook Group named *"The Worthy Goddess Community"*, which is full of an array of talented, wise, wonderful women to collaborate with and share their stories, their gifts and their wisdom. My group specifically gives the Mystics, healers, artists, writers, speakers, and any women in the personal development field, a chance to showcase their gifts and help inspire and collaborate with other women who are also searching for more empowerment and enlightenment.

The Worthy Goddess Community Group allows women to realise that the goddess lives in all of us and she is waiting to shine and spread her "sparkle". I have also just introduced an exclusive VIP membership called *"The Worthy Goddess Sanctuary"*, which provides virtual circles featuring a goddess card of the month, astrological themes including Sun Sign of the Month, intuitive insights, and personalised mini-readings for each member.

Becoming part of a community of women helped me greatly to tap into my true purpose, and provided a whole new level of joy for life. I know now, without a doubt, **magic certainly does happen when women gather in a sacred space.**

Your Path to Community

Being part of communities of women can help you to become a much more fulfilled person, and this is a path that I highly recommend you pursue. One of the most inspiring and connected ways to join a community is through attending women's circles, as they are extremely healing and transformational.

As mentioned, this was something I began to recognise in my 40's. Prior to that time, I had spent most of my life feeling extremely disconnected and not really part of any communities. I have experienced the true power of being part of communities of like-minded heart-centred women, and I now recognise how much of a difference it has made.

I cannot emphasise how important it is to pursue joining a community, and connecting to your soul "tribe" of women. When you do this, you'll understand that there are women out there who will appreciate you and support you. Women that do not judge, compete or compare, but will honour you as you honour and support them.

I really think that many women are lacking these insights, and do not know how important community is, and how it can enrich life in so many ways. The power of women's circles has helped me heal from the pain of being bullied by girls in my youth, and my mistrust of other women which is a huge change.

Finding Your Tribe

It is no secret that for centuries women gathered to connect, support and celebrate each other and, luckily today, many women are realising that becoming part of a tribe of like-minded, heart-centred women is not only nourishing, but can be life-changing.

I understand that women who have never attended a circle might be fearful of what happens there. It does make me chuckle when some think we do really strange things, like running around outside naked and howling at the moon. At the circles I have attended, (and I have now attended quite a few), we do nothing of the sort. The circles that I have attended and now facilitate are open, honest as we break down some barriers, and we are able to experience a whole new level of compassion and respect for each fellow woman.

It's such a lovely way to connect to other women and you'll naturally open up and share some parts of your life. The vibration created will really help you to do this quite organically. Being in a circle is an amazing vehicle for women to be able to share in a non-judgmental, loving and nurturing environment.

In some circumstances, these communities may open up your ability to express yourself and be open about how you really feel. You can say as little or as much as you like, as other women are there to also honour you, including holding space for you and allowing you to have a voice. To sum up one of my circles, or some that I have attended, it is "total nourishment of the mind, body and heart".

Being part of a sacred circle will help you to heal and become conscious of your feelings, learn to trust, have a voice, listen to others without coaching and so much more. It's **not** a group of women getting together to run down men or other people, and it's certainly not a "bitch" session. It's a wonderful opportunity to take off your mask, be completely authentic, and speak your truth without any form of judgement.

It is not permitted, and goes against the ethics and integrity, to discuss anyone else's personal life outside of the circle. Raw emotions and feelings can come up and we need to honour and respect each and every woman in that circle. We do not ever share outside of the circle whatever happens inside. Women's circles are like Las Vegas, *"what happens in the circle, stays in the circle"*.

When you start going to different events and circles it begins to snowball, and before you know it, you are part of this huge amazing community of awesome and divine women, which I call a "collective of deliciousness".

Healing from Past Trauma

If you were like me and bullied at school by other girls, you may still need to heal that wound, otherwise you may never feel completely comfortable with women. You could very well miss out on amazing friendships and connections which would be a shame.

Empowered confident women, who I also refer to as goddesses, do not need to compete or compare with each other, and will celebrate your success as you can celebrate theirs. Once you realise that you just want to be the best version of yourself and shine your own light, you will never be threatened by other women and you will never feel jealous or envious.

If you do, then you know you still have more work to do on yourself, particularly with regard to your own worth. When you really love, honour and appreciate yourself, and know who you are and what you stand for, energetically you will change and then also want the same for other women. It's quite amazing to see the ripple effect that occurs when you give other women permission to do the same.

Be Around People Who Love and Appreciate You

To help you on your path, I really think that it's time to start to be discriminating as to who you spend your time with. If you are still hanging out with girlfriends who drain your energy, are jealous of you, and do not celebrate your awesomeness, then you probably need to do a cleanse of your friends. You also should consider making some new friends that are supportive, loving and inspirational. Once you set this intention, the universe will help you on your path to create more meaningful, heart and soul connections.

I recommend that you start to visualise some fabulous friendships and connections, and make it one of your missions to only be around women that honour you and appreciate you. This is a tremendous feeling when it happens, and you will wonder why it took you so long to do this.

It will start a new quest as you will suddenly want to surround yourself with women who get "YOU", where you have lots of common ground, and celebrate your successes. When you find this, it will be like you have come "home". It may even be a lost memory that is reignited, a memory that existed centuries ago and still resides in your soul. Don't be like me and wait half your life to find true connection and close female friendships.

You do not have to feel alone. Make the choice to open yourself up to new possibilities by putting yourself out there and beginning to meet new people. Not everyone you meet you will connect with; however, when you are open and set clear intentions, you'll find people that you resonate with.

Key Lessons:

- ❖ Understand the power of community and how it can enhance your life in so many ways.
- ❖ Join communities of like-minded women.
- ❖ Women's circles/gatherings can help nourish and help heal your soul, mind and heart, and I highly recommend that you join one or create your own.
- ❖ Your life will be enriched when you surround yourself with inspiring, wise women who celebrate their own success as well as your own.
- ❖ When women gather in sacred space, "magic" transformations occur.

- ❖ Heal from past experiences of bullying and distrust of women, to understanding that many women are amazing and can become great mentors, friends and/or offer support and encouragement.
- ❖ Women connecting with other women can help heal the world – one ripple at a time can make a difference.

"Greatness comes from living with purpose and passion"

– Ralph Marston

Lesson 16

You are Worthy of Living Passionately & On Purpose

I was exceptionally creative as a child and I thought I would be an actress, writer or do something in the arts arena. I was writing and performing plays at the age of four, so it was no surprise that I had a deep desire to work in a creative environment. I also had dreams of completing an Arts Degree and then follow on with some professional acting and theatre training.

My dreams were quickly put on hold when both my grandmother and mother both suggested that I become a secretary, as there were always plenty of jobs in that profession, especially in the 80's. They both were not able to pursue a higher education and didn't really see the value in education. With their influence, secretarial work is exactly what I ended up doing, following the advice from the two women in my life who had the biggest influence on me.

I had a very rocky start to my office career. My first boss turned out to be a sexual predator, and before things got completely out of hand, the next thing I knew I was being dismissed. I remained very silent about his inappropriate behaviour, and it was only when I started writing this book, that I clearly remembered what happened. It was a blessing that I was dismissed as the abuse could have worsened.

I continued to work in offices on and off for 30 years, with quite a few different career changes along the way. **For many years, I never**

really recognised my own worth, and I would continually dismiss my level of capability. I had set up a pattern of *"dumbing myself down"*, which unfortunately is far too common for many women, particularly from my generation.

There have been times in my life where I have changed career direction and moved away from working in office jobs. I have also had some glimpses of living with more purpose and creating a more passionate life. There always seemed to be something else that was stirring deep in my soul and creating restlessness.

Harsh Lessons to Learn

I continued to find jobs that provided good income; however, the search for actual stability and some sort of direction in my life proved to be difficult. I was still feeling an emptiness inside, even when I was earning a good income, paying my bills, and providing a great lifestyle for my daughter and I.

I did feel proud that my daughter did not have to go without. She was given many opportunities, and I was still able to spoil her in many ways. The problem was that I was still on a negative path of going from job-to-job, attracting toxic relationships and **not really grounding myself or recognising what my heart and soul really truly desired**.

Once again, I would have brief moments of living life purposefully and passionately, but then I would lose my way and go back to the old, and then wonder why I wasn't completely happy. I would have many more lessons to learn before I would eventually find my way.

I also had to clear some of that resentment of never having the encouragement to complete a Degree and not having the courage to go after my own dreams. I was starting to realise that it was never too late to work even harder to change my mindset, and to do further healing to breakthrough some ongoing negative behaviour patterns.

I didn't necessarily want to go to University, but there were still some further studies in personal development that were required to align with my higher purpose, and to design a life that I loved.

With my persistence and my deep desire to lead a better life, my life started to change enormously. I met my future husband (#2), and got a secure full-time job. It was at that point that I also knew I needed to keep searching for my actual life purpose, as the stability was great, but I was still not doing the type of work that set my heart on fire.

This was also a time when I started to go to motivational seminars, different events as well as goddess related ones. This really started to help me define what I was searching for and what path I needed to follow to create a more purposeful and passionate life.

Through various communities that I connected with, I was asked to speak at several women's events and gatherings as a guest speaker. I remember being so scared to share my story for the first time, and in hindsight probably a little too intense with far too much story. It was all a learning experience, and it takes practice to learn the art of telling and more importantly, showing my story.

Creating my First Event

In 2015, I created my first unique event, which I called *"Dinner with Goddesses"*. While creating this event, I felt enormous fear, but I refused to allow the fear to stop me. I enjoyed creating the menu, shopping at the market for fresh produce, and then lovingly preparing the food. I put a lot of thought into the content for the night and as per my training, prepared a "running sheet", which was a combination of not only enjoy delicious food surrounded by beauty, but also more deeply sharing heart-centred, authentic conversations, astrological and intuitive insights, all in a healing and sacred space.

I knew at that point that part of my purpose was not only to bring women together in such a beautiful atmosphere, but to help them to feel pampered and in a healing temple where they could feel connected. I wanted each woman to connect to their goddess energy, and to utilise law of attraction principles and self-love practices. I wanted each woman who attended to leave feeling content, calm, grateful, and transformed in some way.

I will never forget the joy I felt at having 14 amazing women around my dining room table at my first event. One of these women was my 22 year-old daughter, which made me so very happy. She also was so proud of me and what I had accomplished, which made my heart sing. The women loved my event, and I observed over the next few years, other women bringing the celebration of food into their own events, and creating more beautiful spaces to gather in.

I have since hosted quite a few events both in Melbourne and Canberra, and I have also started to facilitate bi-monthly circles in my home on a Friday evening or Sunday afternoon. I feel it is such an important movement, to bring communities of women together, again in a sacred, non-judgmental, and supportive environment. It's such a powerful alchemy of divine deliciousness.

Starting any new business is challenging, and vision and branding can seem unclear in those first few years. It was only in 2017 that I started to really develop clarity on my brand and the services that I wanted to offer. After getting married, I decided that my name would be my brand, and JoWorthy.Com was launched with a fresher, more authentic feel. The Worthy Goddess was still used for my FB Groups, and an exclusive membership program is in the process of being developed.

Writing and publishing this book, inspirational speaking, and offering luxury retreats for women will be the new products and services I will provide. I continue to facilitate women's circles as this work I believe is so valuable. I am also working on an exciting new online program, and workshops that align with the lessons in this book. I am creating Love Worthy Affirmation cards, and love, abundance and passion potions that will be available to purchase individually or as part of my online program. My creativity has been on fire, and I am loving my new direction.

The sense of joy and passion I started to feel was like no other I had experienced previously. I was a woman who, for many years, did not really connect to my purpose. I put others wishes and dreams first, wasted too much time wanting to be "perfect", and was too focused on what other people thought of me, rather than concentrating on loving myself and not worrying or putting unnecessary energy into people who do not matter.

I had been living in mediocrity and ignoring all my wisdom, talents and gifts, and then wondering why I felt so lost and unfulfilled. When you connect to your true purpose and you are actually living it, your sense of usefulness, your drive, your passion and that fire in your belly will light you up each and every day. You will feel more alive, more vibrant, and realise why you used to feel so much fatigue and boredom. **Connecting to your purpose is one of the main ingredients for leading a magnificent life**.

As soon as I started on this new path, I was in a beautiful flow and I then knew deeply that I was living purposely. I had a new clarity and an enormous sense of pride, joy and peace were starting to fill my heart and soul, and it felt so damn good! I was also starting to understand I was able to fuel my work through the pain, torment and suffering of my past experiences. I knew I could help other women not to make the same mistakes, and I could guide and help them transform their own lives.

Becoming a Change-Maker

"Be the change you want to see in the world"
Gandhi

A huge part of my purpose or my mission was definitely to start leading by example, being a "change-maker", a true leader, one able to make a huge difference and help as many women as possible. I wanted, through my story and my life experiences, to demonstrate to women that they should never give up on themselves, and they can finally break the cycle of abusive relationships, and learn to love, honour, and cherish themselves.

Your Path to Living Passionately And On Purpose

Living a life that is passionate and one that you absolutely love will change your life exponentially. We are not born to live a boring, complacent or lack-lustre life. You are deserving of living the best possible life and to be the very best version of you. You want to wake up every morning not just happy to be alive, but to be full of hope, wonder, and joy. When you wake up you want to feel grateful to be alive.

Many of us take the difficult path, not believing in our abilities and making second rate decisions. We are not in flow and we end up feeling frustrated and unhappy. When you do find that flow, it's a huge clue that you are on the right path, but how many times do we stay on a path that is against our flow? How many times do we put our dreams on hold, and prioritise other people's needs, rather than giving ourselves the same privilege?

It is wise to not avoid that deep stirring within, the talents that you have been born with and are destined to develop. We are all born with our own individual gifts that are just waiting to be explored, and once we do this the universe will be cheering us on, and new "miraculous" doors will be opened.

When you a living passionately, you are far less burdened by the strains and challenges of life, and you will feel much happier. You will suffer less disease in your body and you will have so much more energy. You will feel a deep sense of joy, and know deep down in your heart and soul that it's the right path. Your body, heart and mind will thank you!

Lack of Self-Worth

One of the main problems with creating a passionate life, is that when you suffer low self-worth, your life will be a struggle, and you'll take the more challenging but mediocre path. You are not listening to your inner-guidance and may feel depleted, depressed and bored with your life. You even stop doing the things that bring you the most joy due to your lethargy and complacency, and a part of you may have sadly given up, and even feel worthless. This is exactly how I felt, until I started to make necessary changes to lead a more purposeful life.

I know from experience that it's very easy to go completely off course when we are suffering, and our vision can be clouded. Life will seem so much harder when we are disconnected from our true purpose and, quite often, we will spend our days going through the motions, aware that something doesn't feel right, but without having the energy or the inclination to make the change.

Whether it be your relationships, your career or any other aspect of your life, if you suffer low self-worth, you will continue to make second rate decisions, underestimate your abilities, and be unable to connect to your magnificence. This is where you really need to take control of your life, be totally accountable, and make the necessary changes.

We are not a tree, we can move, and we can change if our life is not where we want it to be. We need to face our fears, connect to our courage and know that change is inevitable if we are to expand and grow into a better version of ourselves. Be brave, beautiful women, and connect deeply to your desires, dreams, and wishes. **Go after what you deserve, which is an amazing passionate life. You have the power to create this!**

Momentum of Change

Sometimes we can get so caught up in our "pain and fears" that this becomes our comfort zone, our "normal". Once you take that initial step of breaking that negative cycle, and bring back some "fire into your belly", it may be enough motivation to start a huge momentum of change. If you can get to this stage, you will notice what a big difference it can make to your attitude and your energy. You will start to feel that life has a PURPOSE once again, and you have a reason for jumping out of bed in the morning, feeling excited that you have a deeper reason for your existence.

You could be getting to a stage in your life where you are frequently questioning and wondering why there seems to be a huge void. If you are experiencing these feelings, it's actually a good thing, so you can first understand that you need to make changes, before any changes can occur.

You will then know that it's time for you to get really clear on what you want in your life, as well as what you don't want. Once you have a clear plan and you are in flow, the universe can then begin to work with you to create a much more passionate life.

Think about some of the times in your life where you haven't followed your dreams and desires. It may have been related to your career, or you might have also experienced a similar situation to me, in that you listened to a parent regarding what direction to take in relation to your studies and/or career path.

It can be difficult during our childhoods, as we are extremely vulnerable and we often take advice from either a parent, teacher or someone else in authority. Particularly, if we are also suffering from low self-worth, we can often lack a lot of our own inner direction, and we do not have the courage to pursue our own dreams and goals.

Don't Give Up on Your Dreams

We cannot change our past, but we can most definitely change our present and our future. If you didn't follow your true path, the good news is: **it's never too late.** I have known people well into their later years, finally pursuing things that they have always loved and utilising the talents that they were either born with or developed.

It's very common for many women to put their own dreams on hold and put the needs of their partner first. You **cannot live with regret, things do happen for a reason, but we also need to be fully conscious and not lose sight of our own dreams and wishes.**

Within a relationship, you need to compromise; however, there also needs to be a balance. If you are always the one compromising, then maybe you are just settling, and placing your own needs on hold. Like me, maybe there is a theme in your own life, where you have compromised your own true deep desires. Once you recognise this, you can make the necessary changes, so you won't keep repeating the same limiting pattern.

Determining your Life Purpose

If you are feeling lost about what your true purpose is, I highly recommend that you utilise different modalities to help guide you on your path. I have used astrology, goddess cards, and my own intuitive insights — not only for my own personal development, but also for my clients.

We have so many powerful modalities available to assist us in our search, and I highly recommend that you allow yourself to be open to exploring different options and what appeals to you. I also learned from hand analysis, that my purpose was to be an author, a speaker in the spotlight, carrying a healing message to the masses. That was a huge "light bulb" moment.

My wish is for you to live a life that is purposeful and passionate. Life is far too short to be just going through the motions and wondering if this is all there is. We can easily get stuck in a rut, we forget our true path, and we forget that we are worth so much more than a mediocre life. It's now time for you to consider how you can make your life far more magnificent.

Whether this be where you live, who you have relationships with, or what job choices you make, you need to stop and think and even ask the question "Is this going to make my heart sing?" and "Is this decision going to make me happy?". Remember to stay focused on *your* vision of happiness, not how others define it.

It doesn't matter what you do in your life, but ensure you are making a difference, and that you are passionate about what you are doing. If you can then combine this with making a positive difference to other people's lives and help them to improve theirs, then I believe you are definitely living "on purpose".

It takes courage to make changes, and it takes a "leap of faith", and trust in your intuition. Remember, life is short, and before you know it you may be in circumstances you actually hate, and suddenly ten or more years have gone by. Stop and think about what you would like to do and make the necessary changes. Don't keep doing things that bring you no joy and are depleting your energy and your spirit.

Find People who Inspire You

There are so many wonderful stories of people conquering adversity and the only difference is that they changed their mindset. They didn't allow their pasts to define their futures, and they had a very clear vision of what they wanted to achieve, while trusting and believing in themselves. I suggest that you read about other people's adversities, as it will give you hope as to what you too can achieve.

> *"Do not die with the music still in you"*
> *Wayne Dyer*

Not all of us are going to want to affect thousands of people; however, the point is that your true purpose might become clearer through all of your suffering. Think about what you have been through in your own life, and how you can teach other people some of the lessons that you have learned, as this will give you huge insight and clues as to what your own purpose is.

Your pain is often your purpose

Key Lessons:

- ❖ Break the cycle of your ancestors and their expectations.
- ❖ Take the time to really think about your own desires and goals. Write these down, create a plan and stay on your path.
- ❖ Display courage and resilience to make the necessary changes to enhance your life.
- ❖ Don't just take the first opportunity offered to you – think about it and ask yourself is this really what I am searching for?
- ❖ Stop making decisions based on someone else's dream and therefore forgetting about yours.
- ❖ Listen and trust your intuition and your "inner-knowing".

"There comes a time when nothing is meaningful except surrendering to love"

– Rumi

Lesson 17

You are Worthy of Surrendering

My First Bali Awakening

It was during this first trip to beautiful Bali that deeper healing and releasing some more "suffering" was going to take place. Interestingly enough, I wasn't consciously aware that I was still holding onto unresolved pain, after all the work that I had done on myself to this point. My revelations were going to prove to be profound.

It was like another layer of pain was about to be healed; some of which had laid in my heart and soul for many years. It's quite amazing how it can feel that we are just coasting along in life and we think that everything is okay. We think we have healed from our past pain, and we think we have got it all figured out.

Like many of us, I certainly had my share of adversity, and I was proud that I had changed and allowed myself to become a much better version of me. I was far happier, healthier, and consciously creating a wonderful life. I was in love with my man and feeling like I was experiencing many "sweet spots". On this holiday in Bali, I realised that I needed further layer of healing so that I could experience even more love and happiness.

It was in this magical place, where I would finally be able to open up my heart fully, and heal that part of me that was still hurting and untrusting. I started asking myself "Am I finally able to fully surrender?". This was HUGE, and being able to fully surrender to love and be loved would be massive relief to both myself and my man.

A Life Changing Holiday

It was September 2016, and I was just about to embark on what could only be described as a life-changing holiday. Mr Worthy and I were going to Palm Cove in Queensland for my niece's wedding, so we decided to plan a great holiday in Bali for seven nights after the wedding.

Little did I know, this would be a trip that would remain in my heart and soul forever. It would be this holiday that would allow me to finally surrender. Bali is truly magnificent, and I didn't realise that the energy was going to be such a high vibration. This energy allowed me to heal at a deeper level and my creative juices began to flow in such incredible ways.

I felt so blessed that I was able to connect at such a deep level to my creativity, which allowed me to start my writing once again. There were only minor moments throughout my adult life where I truly connected to my absolute "passions" and I was actually amazed and relieved that my new addiction was writing. I started to become obsessed with it, to the point that I just wanted to write every spare moment that I had. This was actually the start of my process of becoming truly serious about writing this very book!

After experiencing Bali for the first time, I now know why so many people go there and search for more meaning and deeper spiritual awakenings. Energetically, Bali is a very special place, and I think that if you are open to receiving, it will provide you many chances to open your heart and soul and go deeper within. It is now no surprise to me that so many people facilitate retreats in beautiful Bali, "*The Island of the Gods*".

I have now taken quite a few trips to Bali since September 2016, and it has become my most favourite place in the world to visit, my spiritual & creative haven. There is no doubt that with each visit, my heart and soul has opened up that bit more, and enhanced my spiritual understanding on many deeper levels. This has allowed me to feel a lot more peace within myself, and consequently allowed me to also share my work on a much deeper basis.

My breakthroughs have been incredible, and Bali is a place I highly recommend you visit if you want to flourish on a spiritual level and become more awakened. Of course, in addition you'll also get tropical warm weather, awesome food, and fabulously friendly, amazing locals and culture.

Admittedly, some people prefer to go to Bali to party and/or just relax, and that is a personal choice. But Bali offers so much more if you are open to growth and really want to go deeper with your healing and become even more empowered and centred.

Trust your Intuition and Allow Yourself to be Divinely Guided

Whilst in Bali, serendipity was at its finest, as I had the great privilege of being introduced to another healer; a man who usually only sees locals and existing clients/students. I was fortunate that one of my friends in Australia knew this healer very well, and had been one of his students for many years. This allowed me to secure an appointment on the day we were leaving Ubud, a stunning area of central Bali.

I strongly believe that things like this never happen by coincidence, as the teacher appeared in the very instance that I was ready to meet him. This healer helped calm my restless spirit, and aided me to be able to fully commit to my man, clearing away any of the "debris" that may have been preventing me from doing so in the past.

I understand that many will be sceptical about so called "gurus" or "healers", and even with my own spiritual understandings, I can still be a little critical at times, when my logical mind will overtake my inner-knowing. However, after my personal experience and what changed so profoundly within me, I am now a complete believer that there are some great healers available to us. **We must first be open to healing to occur and then allow ourselves to be divinely guided**.

There was certainly a shift after this healing and the energetic vibration of Bali, I believed enhanced my experience. I felt for the first time in my life that my heart had actually fully opened and this was an incredible feeling, as there was no more "hiding out", and pretending all was okay.

I felt a complete sense of peace and freedom, like I had released myself from my own emotional prison. I felt that with my heart open I could love so much more – give love, be love and just LOVE with a whole open heart. I also felt that I had won the lottery on an emotional level!

My healing journey had been an extremely long one, but still, one so worth pursuing. To be able to move forward in my life, and learn to love and to accept love was huge. For most of my life I had created such torture within my heart being unable to do this, and here I was, a woman 51 years of age experiencing this enormous breakthrough. Thank goodness my man was patient, as we had been together for over six years before I could feel that love, and accept his love, and then commit fully to him.

My commitment to "Mr. Worthy" increased to a whole new level, so much so that after that fated Bali trip in September, and upon returning to Australia, I then decided it was time to accept his marriage proposal. He had been patient with me, and had wanted to marry me for quite a few years; however, I was hesitant and fearful about marriage because of my past traumas.

It was only when I returned from Bali that I then realised I loved him completely, and it was high time I committed fully and trusted my heart. It was at that very point in our relationship that we started planning our wedding, as I accepted that it was finally time to SURRENDER, trust, and marry again.

My journey had been immense to reach this point in my life, however without a doubt it was so worth the work on repairing my wounds and being open to deeper healing. It was worth affirming I was deserving of a beautiful man in my life, that treated me with the utmost respect and loved and adored me. It was worth putting up with the family challenges, working on both our problems and staying loyal and supportive to one another. It was so worth feeling Love Worthy!

Your Path to Surrendering

Have you felt so disillusioned with surrendering to love once again to the point where you don't even want to try? Has your heart been damaged to the point where surrendering to a subsequent partner fully was a challenge, and so you stayed in avoidance mode?

Perhaps like me, you have also experienced a lot of pain around your relationships, and you are still hanging onto to some of this suffering and not fully surrendering or committing to your partner. Perhaps you are even avoiding a relationship all together because your heart is still hurting? Maybe it is time for you to surrender.

My wish is that you also choose to go deeper with your healing, allowing yourself to forgive and accept what has happened is in the past, and that you do not have to keep holding onto that pain any longer. Know that you can release the hurt and betrayal.

I would also love for you to get to a stage where you feel that immense freedom, happiness and enormous peace that you will receive when you fully surrender, releasing yourself from your own "emotional prison" once and for all. **You need to know that you can heal, you can forgive and can surrender to LOVE.**

It can take a lot of dedication and devotion to know that you are completely worthy of healing. It's a journey you must embark on if you want to live a love worthy and magnificent life.

I also suggest that you are completely open to finding the right "teachers" and mentors, and start asking for divine guidance when you are ready and open. I believe the teacher will "miraculously" appear, and will support you in ways you didn't think possible. **Trust your heart and allow yourself to be divinely guided, as this is where real magic can occur.**

Meditation – Be Open and Allow for Guidance

Sometimes it's difficult to know where to start, and we can become overwhelmed at the mere thought of calming our minds and asking for guidance. This is why I highly recommend meditation. It's a great tool to stop, pause, breathe and reflect. It's also the perfect setting to ask your angels, your guides, your god or goddesses (use what is comfortable for you), for support and divine guidance. I believe they are there waiting to receive your permission so they can help you. You need to ask and you need to trust.

Create an Altar

Create a beautiful altar that you can meditate in front of, with candles, incense, aromatherapy oils, crystals, fresh flowers etc., and have this as your sacred place. While you are at your "temple", you can really connect to your inner-wisdom and start to trust your intuition. It's a power we all have, we just need to create the space and take the time to truly connect, and allow our lives to be much more in flow.

Meditation / Relaxation Exercise

I prefer to lay down for this exercise, so find a comfortable place to lie with some cushions and a throw rug (use your yoga mat if you have one to make it more comfortable for you). Light your candles, play some lovely relaxing music, burn or vaporise your favourite pure essential oils, take three deep breaths and exhale loudly after each breath, feel your whole self unwinding as you work your way up relaxing each part of your body, starting at your toes and finishing at the top of your head.

As you are doing this, breathe out your fears and stresses and breathe in love energy. It's at this point of relaxation where it's the perfect time to ask for guidance and support from our higher beings.

You can customise your request for guidance to what is right for you personally, however here is one of my suggestions:

Dear guardian angels, I am feeling lost and I also require deeper healing so I can release myself from my past hurt and live a more amazing life. Please guide me and help me on my path so I can live a life that is for my highest purpose. Please help me to release anything that is no longer serving me.

Laying in your relaxed state, breathe out any fear, shame, or guilt from your body and breathe in more love. You may find that once you are in this relaxed state that you receive some answers to some of your problems. Once you come out of your meditative state, I suggest that you have a journal beside you so that you can write down your insights and refer to them to assist you on your current path.

It's okay if you do not consciously receive anything at this point, as at minimum you have energetically opened the channel for extra guidance, and you may find that you are divinely guided in many subtle ways. It will not even be a surprise if all of sudden you meet a healer/teacher/mentor that will assist you greatly and provide further guidance to you. Be open to this happening and trust the process, without becoming too logical thereby blocking any messages that you might receive.

In relation to meditation exercises, you can download from a huge choice on the internet. There are also some fabulous guided mediations available to you these days, which I recommend for beginners. These guided meditations are often a great place to start, especially if you're have trouble shutting off the inner chatter that constantly wants to interfere with your relaxation.

It's really important that you start the conscious path of healing so you can lead a more delicious and amazing life. As outlined above, meditation is a wonderful way to start to become more self-aware. It's also a time that is just for you, and allows you to release anything that is not serving you. Asking for guidance or merely relaxing the mind and body will help you to think more clearly and connect to your inner-wisdom.

We are very lucky to have so many healers around to assist, so I recommend that you become curious and start asking for recommendations. Experiment with different modalities, to work out what is right for you. I have found that if you keep asking for guidance, the right people will come into your life as if it's a "miracle". **Be open to miracles, be open to be divinely guided, and trust your instincts.**

I personally have tried many different modalities, and as mentioned there are many healers available to help you, but firstly, you need to be willing to change and be open to healing. You could meet the best healer in the world, but you need to be able to receive and really want to change. I really believe "once you ask you shall receive".

There are also many people out there, who like me, were searching for deeper healing, meaning and love, and they found the exact person to help them. *"Eat Pray Love"* by Elizabeth Gilbert is a perfect and well-known example of a woman who was searching, and she also found her guru in Bali, as I suspect many people have done over the years.

There are many other scared places in the world that have a higher energetic presence for healing. Hawaii, parts of South America and India are also apparently known for profound healing. I highly recommend that you choose a place that you prefer, and make plans to go there with the intention of deeper healing and enlightenment. Not only will you experience fun, adventure, and new cultures, but you may also find that your heart heals that little bit more, and that you can finally also surrender to love.

Retreating

There are so many amazing transformational retreats available to us, and even retreating for a few days can help change your life in remarkable and surprising ways. I have become a "retreat junkie", and have had many amazing and life-long memories formed while attending retreats.

This includes many breakthroughs, plus the deeper healing, and life-long connections made with other women who were present. There is a wide choice of retreats held all over the world, with amazing and talented heart centred women running them, and with other awesome women attending to connect to and learn from.

You are Your Best Investment

I certainly believe that healing your heart and soul will be one of the best investments that you can ever make, and will allow you to love you more. In saying this, I also believe **it takes a conscious person to want to heal, and it takes courage, persistence and a strong belief that you are worth a happier life.**

Once you can reveal all that needs to be healed, you are well on your way to deeper healing, which can result in further contentment and love in your heart. Once you start to release your fears around love, you can then start to surrender more fully to endless possibilities of creating your own "love story". Most importantly, I firmly believe love needs to be felt within, so work on you first and foremost and then watch the magic unfold as your start to recognise your value and your own worth.

Once you are able to do this, your life will become so much "richer" on a mind, body and soul level. I truly believe that this is what the universe is waiting for you to do. When you realise that the universe has your back and wants you to open your heart, open your arms and release all that pain holding you back, you can then truly start to live a deliciously divine life.

Key Lessons:

- ❖ Be open to further healing, allow, accept and trust the process.
- ❖ Go to places that have a higher vibration so that the healing experience is even more powerful.
- ❖ Know that you can learn to trust, forgive and love with a full, open heart once again.
- ❖ Create a sacred space in your home and meditate regularly so you connect to your higher-self, your guides/angels/god/goddesses. Ask for guidance and support.
- ❖ Be persistent with your healing and keep going on your journey and know that you deserve complete happiness.
- ❖ Do not give up and never give up on yourself. Know that you can heal, forgive and you can LOVE and SURRENDER.

"Words are not enough to express the unconditional love that exists between a mother and a daughter"

– Caitlin Houston

Lesson 18

You are Worthy of Unconditional Love

When we develop unconditional love for ourselves, it is one of the most wonderful things that we can create and this is when real "miracles" occur. In addition to our own unconditional love towards ourselves, I also feel that we are quite often loved or love unconditionally when it comes to our parents and most definitely our own children.

For me personally, with all the suffering that I have encountered, I feel blessed that the love I feel towards my own mother and my daughter is unconditional love. My love for them both is enormous, and one that I will never feel complacent about. This is a love that I appreciate tremendously.

My mother, Sylvia, very sadly passed away in March 2017. I must admit that I did not always see my mother as much as I would have liked to, but nevertheless, I always had a deep-seated love for her, and I wish we had more time together. Moving interstate did not help with the ability to see each other, and phone calls were never the same as seeing my dear mum face-to-face and getting one of her amazing heart-felt hugs. My heart aches for her and I miss her physical presence.

My Daughter was a Blessing

It was in 1993 when I gave birth to my own daughter, I realised the love for my own mother went to different levels, and I felt that I loved my mother unconditionally at this point. It was when I discovered just how precious it is to be a parent, and the love we feel for our own child is immeasurable.

I felt so very blessed when my daughter was born, and knew very quickly that motherhood was another amazing aspect of unconditional love. Even when my life went to absolute crap, it was my daughter who helped to keep me going, stopped me from giving up, and gave me the determination to get my life back on track.

My daughter (26 years old at the time of publishing), often expresses immense gratitude, and actually thanks me for all the delicious meals and the lovely homes that I consistently provided over those years of instability and craziness. I am proud of the young woman she has become, including her strength, resilience, and the fact that she is a smart, loyal, and very savvy young woman.

It was approximately 2011, when we discovered my incestuous child abusing ex-husband and father of our daughter had passed away from heart failure. I actually found out from the Child Support Agency, via correspondence informing me that my child support payments had stopped due to his passing. It was a terrible way to find out that he had passed away, and his family didn't even give us the respect of contacting us, which they could have done easily.

I also felt very distressed for my daughter, as she was not able to have any closure with her father. She wasn't even able (or invited) to attend his funeral. I think his family just wanted us to disappear and forget that we existed, as they did not want to be reminded of what their son had done.

Motherhood has helped me build resilience, and has shown me what unconditional love truly is in the purest of forms. There is no doubt that parenting can be tough at times, but it can also be one of the most rewarding experiences, teaching us so much about ourselves, our capacity to love, nurture, protect and guide the most precious thing of all — our children.

Big Life Events

2017 was certainly a year of big life events, with a mixture of beautiful blessings, alongside huge loss and grief to deal with. The blessing was I was getting married in May, yet my enormous grief was due to my mother's passing who passed away on Sunday 19 March 2017, in Melbourne. She had suffered several strokes, with the last stroke being fatal.

Those last 24 hours prior to her passing, my sister had called me to say that I needed to get to the hospital as soon as possible, as Mum had suffered a stroke after her operation and was fighting for her life. Of course, I immediately got on a flight to Melbourne, hoping and praying that she didn't pass away prior to me seeing her and hugging her one last time. That was the longest flight I have ever experienced, from Canberra to Melbourne.

When I arrived and saw Mum laying in the hospital bed after her first stroke, I vividly remember the desperate look in her eyes. It felt and looked as if she was pleading with my sister, that she no longer wanted to be here, and that it was her time to leave this physical world. My sister also deeply felt this as well.

Mum did hang in there for another night, however the hospital rang my sister at 6am on Sunday morning to inform us that we needed to come into the hospital immediately, as Mum had suffered yet another stroke, and this one was probably going to be fatal. Two hours later my beautiful mother joined the angels to embark on another journey.

Those first few days with my brother and sister, my partner and extended family were like a blur. The worst thing is, when you are going through so much grief, but you still have to keep going as there are so many things to organise. You cannot just crawl up in a ball of emotion and shut off from the world, even though you want to.

We all had to come to terms with no longer being able to call Mum, and having those long chats with her giving updates about our lives. Not that our mother could ever be replaced, but my sister and I started calling each other more, and took comfort from each other. Mum will be shining down on us, and I'm so happy that my sister and I have become even closer.

Mum's passing was heart-wrenching and the emotional pain that we feel when it's someone we love so deeply, is way beyond words. I just knew that my heart had never ached so much and that my life would never be the same ever again. My mother was my main source of support in the family, almost like my champion quietly in the background, and she was one of my biggest loves throughout my life. I had to try and live without her physical presence and knew there would never be anyone in my whole universe that could ever come close to replacing her.

Mum had been sick on and off for many years, but I **never** expected her to die at 74. The ridiculous thing was, at this time Mum had gone into hospital to have a standard shoulder operation, nothing too serious. Admittedly, this operation had been put on hold as Doctors had doubts about whether she would survive another operation because of her ill health. Unfortunately, Mum was also a heavy smoker, and prior to the other operations that she had over the years, she would usually give up smoking a few weeks prior to any surgery; however, on this occasion she had kept on smoking.

I remember three weeks after she had passed, that my emotions were even more intense, ranging from extreme sadness, to sobbing, to disbelief that she had gone. There were some days, I simply felt numb and would just go through the motions, and others where I strongly felt the grief in my stomach and in my heart, and tears would often well up in my eyes.

At this time, I was not working, which was a blessing, as I don't know how I would have gotten through a normal working day in those first few weeks without breaking down. I did have a wedding to plan, so in some ways I was able to divert my attention to a really wonderful event in my life, which was a welcome distraction from the intense grief.

There were some days where I felt the full awareness of my Mum's passing, and my emotions would be so very raw with tears running down my cheeks. I tried to deal with the enormity that I would never return to her home or be able to physically see her and hug her. I would no longer be able to share endless cups of tea or a meal together, give her a cuddle, or even pick up the phone to see how she was and hear her voice.

Even though Mum and Dad had been divorced for years, Dad also felt her loss deeply. Mum was the mother of his children and in his own way he had loved her. I did at least have one parent living and even through all the questions in regards to my Mum & Dad's relationship, I did still in fact love my father.

I could not envisage how losing Mum would be a whole new level of grief. The intensity of the pain actually took me by surprise. Even though I knew from a spiritual perspective she would always reside in my heart, and I had only lost her in the physical sense, the fact that I would never see her again in that form was so very hard to believe.

I think anyone who has lost their mother (or father), would agree that losing your parent is something you never really recover from. You learn to accept that they are now around you in a spiritual form, instead of a physical form.

The love for my mother is deep and everlasting and every day I miss her, every day I love her and every day I talk to her and send her so much love. My only relief is that I know she is free from all the illness, the physical and emotional pain that she suffered, and that she is now at peace. Even with my spiritual beliefs, I still miss her physical presence, and often forget and go to call her, before I remember that she is gone.

Mum's Sickness

There were many times throughout my childhood where I witnessed my mother suffering from sickness, and many times she was in hospital recovering from an array of operations. It was because of her ongoing illness and dealing with such unhappiness in her own life, she was very disconnected from our school activities and other parts of our lives.

Also, to add to both my parent's grief, they lost their fourth child in 1968, a son, due to extreme brain damage. He sadly passed away after only 5 days. Mum nearly died at this time as well as the baby, so I am so thankful that she survived. I realise I was luckier than many, as was able to have a mother until I was 52 years of age.

At this point in my life I am not yet a grandmother; however, I still continue to have a close relationship with my daughter. Our mother/daughter bond is never broken, it is strong, it is a constant love, and it is definitely love that is pure and unconditional.

Your Path to Unconditional Love

There is so much gratitude in my heart and I do feel fortunate that my mother loved me unconditionally. Additionally, I feel so blessed that I have a daughter whom I also love unconditionally. I truly hope that you also feel unconditional love from your loved ones. Most importantly I hope that you are creating unconditional love for yourself, although loving oneself can be the most difficult journey.

We all deserve to feel unconditionally loved in our lives and to love unconditionally in turn. I am extremely lucky that I felt this with Mum, as I know there are women who don't feel this way, and if it has caused a lot of suffering, may require further healing in regard to their relationship with their own mother.

With regard to my situation, my Mum may not have been the perfect mother, although of course no one is perfect. I still had to go through some of my healing and forgiveness practices towards my relationship with her. I recognise that she could be a little critical at times, particularly when I was growing up; however, I now realise that she was only like this because she was so hard and critical on herself.

The overriding factor was that I knew that she loved me and I felt that deeply, regardless of her critical nature. She had her own fears and insecurities to deal with. As a mother, I knew that she could mutually feel my pain, and that she genuinely wanted me to be happy.

For many of us, loving our parents unconditionally can be challenging at times. We may have to release the judgements, release the criticisms, practice forgiveness and start to love with a pure heart. I believe there is no better love than unconditional love, and everyone is completely worthy of this type of love.

The Passing of a Loved One

Having a loved one pass over, is probably one of the hardest things that you ever have to deal with in regard to processing and navigating your way through intense grief. The grief can be enormous, regardless of what your spiritual beliefs are, and even now, after over two years since her passing, I still find it difficult to comprehend that dear Mum is gone. It's certainly a great reminder to love the people in your life with a big open heart, and tell them frequently how much you love and appreciate them.

Get Over the Grudges

It's also extremely wise to **not** hold grudges with your loved ones, and learn to forgive them if you think they have done you wrong. Understand that no one is perfect, and most people are doing the best they can do under their own circumstances. This also includes Mum, as I know that she did the best she could with what she had and what she was dealing with.

Please don't wait to make amends if you have had a falling out with a loved one. Now is the time to forgive, don't wait until after they have passed. I suggest that you don't waste another day being bitter, as this will only affect your happiness. Really forgive, and know that with all their own fears, insecurities and sufferings, they may not always have been able to be the best parent they wanted to be.

Forgiveness can be a huge ask in some instances, particularly if they have done something that seems unforgivable. Always know that forgiveness is not really about them anyway, it is actually about you learning to forgive yourself and being able to free yourself from the suffering that may well be weighing you down and preventing you from being the best version of you.

With regard to Mum, I could complain that she wasn't very supportive at certain times in my life. I could complain that she never got involved with school activities, that she didn't come and visit me when I moved out of home, oh the list could go on. But the fact is, she was doing the best she could, and she had a lot of pain to contend with, both physically and mentally, and I just needed to appreciate her for her love and her kindness.

I did a lot of this clearing when I was in my 20's, as I used to feel resentful and wonder why I didn't have parents that were more supportive and stronger role models. Once again, in my 30's, Mum's unconditional love toward me was extremely evident when she stood by me when I was at my lowest point. Mum may not have always been around for me, but I knew that she always loved and adored me. I am eternally thankful, and know that I am luckier than many.

If necessary, it is time to clear your own heart of any bitterness and appreciate all that your parent/s did for you, and not what they didn't do. Parenting is a tough job, and none of us are ever perfect. When you throw into the mix that they also had to deal with various challenges, losses, betrayals, abuses, fears and insecurities, you can start to understand that it's tough to be a parent.

My Spiritual Beliefs

Prior to Mum passing away, I always believed in the after-life and that we never really die as our soul lives on for eternity. Initially, when Mum passed, I still had these beliefs; however, I felt the enormous grief blocked any communication I thought I could have with Mum. It was only quite a few months after she passed that I felt I could sense my mother in spirit, and that she was somehow communicating with me.

This in itself gave me some peace, knowing that Mum didn't really die and that she would always be alive in a soul form. I would start having conversations with Mum and would tune into her messages, and felt her presence and guidance very strongly.

I still have my days when the grief is intense, and I miss Mum so much, but knowing that she will always love me and always be with me, is extremely comforting. There is still not a day that goes by that

I don't miss her. I want to honour Mum and the unconditional love she had for me on a daily basis. I am not sure what your spiritual beliefs are, and they are personal for each and every one of us. All I can say is that my beliefs gave me a lot of comfort.

Key Lessons

- Know that grief is a personal journey and how you deal with it will differ from someone else. You cannot compare your grief journey with another.
- Honour your feelings and if you want to cry, just cry, and let out your emotions.
- Realise that your life will be different when you lose a parent (or any loved one), but you will eventually adjust your life.
- Begin the process of feeling their love around you, and know that they are now at peace and happy, and that you never lose their love, as that's eternal.
- Start to talk to your loved ones, regardless of your beliefs, as it can bring some comfort to you (I look at Mum's photo nearly every day and talk with her).
- Your loved one will want you to be happy, so don't deny yourself this happiness. You can still be grieving, but it's also okay to have some happy moments. Do not feel guilty about this.
- Be even more gentle on yourself particularly during that very raw grief. Increase your self-care and spend more time on your own, journaling your feelings and releasing the sorrow.
- You don't have to put on an act and pretend all is okay. Tell people that you have just lost a loved one and that you are dealing with it the best way you can.

Within three days of Mum passing, I wrote this letter:

My dear Mama,

My heart breaks as you have now left this physical world,

I miss your voice, our chats and I miss your big hugs and endless cups of tea we shared.

You lived a life with so much pain, so I am happy for you that you are no longer suffering, and that you have now reunited with many other "angels", your dad, your mum, your baby boy, your brothers and your beloved Denis.

I hope you are now soaring high with all these angels, no more pain and feeling so much love and peace that you so deserve.

Most days I feel your presence around me, and I know that you are not really "gone".

I will always remember that look in your eye, the night prior to you passing, it was like "Please let me go". You were so over all the pain and suffering and you wanted so much for your next journey to begin.

My mama there are so many memories of you over the past 52 years of my life –

My mama my first love.

The woman who always loved me unconditionally no matter what.

A simplistic, practical and beautiful humble woman,

who loved to show her love for her family through her cooking, and who never asked for much except the love and support of her family.

To be honest Mama, some days my heart aches for you,

some days I just feel numb.

Some days it just feels surreal that you are no longer on this planet.

Some days I just feel flat and I am wallowing in grief, wondering how I will get through without you.

I know you will be smiling down on me at my wedding next month, so happy that I have finally found a good man to love and be loved by, however I will miss your presence so much.

Now my wish is that you are now soaring high surrounded by huge amounts of love and peace and with all the other "angels".

You are gone physically,

But never ever forgotten,

You are always in my heart and soul for eternity,

Every day I will love you,

Every day I will talk to you in spirit,

Every day I will honour you and love you.

Your "baby" girl - "Flossy"

> *"Commitment is what transforms a promise into reality"*
>
> – Abraham Lincoln

Lesson 19

You are Worthy of Commitment

What a journey I have had, particularly with regard to my personal relationships. I think many people would have given up on love and relationships if they had experienced some of the things that I have. Imagine how sad it would have been if I had done this, and not kept my faith that I could meet my life partner and fall in love once again.

The last ten years together has been a huge journey, and one where we were able to overcome a lot of challenges and difficulties. It's during the difficult times that your commitment to each other is highlighted. I love Marilyn Monroe's words: *"if you cannot accept me at my worst, you do not deserve to have me at my best"*. I wholeheartedly believe this is true. When the going gets tough, that is the time when you really need to stay true to one another, and support and love each other even more.

Empty-Nesters

My husband and I currently reside in Canberra as "empty nesters", as our three adult children reside in our home town of Melbourne. Living together as a couple without children has created more harmony in our relationship, and I feel our home life is much more balanced and less stressful. Of course, I still miss the children and our regular dinners and catch-ups. I also miss hanging out with my daughter, but we both make an effort to visit one another and spend valuable time together.

After many challenges and a few heartbreaking moments, I love the fact that my husband now gets on very well with my daughter, and I don't feel caught between them both any longer. I also love the fact that the boys have now accepted me as their stepmother and a major part of their Dad's life, and consequently, their lives as well. To anyone else dealing with blended family challenges, my advice is to remain patient and don't give up on the possibility of being accepted.

So Much Gratitude

My husband and I are in the process of creating a wonderful life together, full of travel adventures, great family and friends in both Melbourne, Canberra, Queensland and Bali! We both have good jobs/incomes, and we have created a beautiful home together. I also have created a wonderful business which my husband is very supportive of and since running my own business I am so much more fulfilled as a person.

I have always been grateful for what I have and not what I have done, however these days I have so much more to be grateful for. I have always utilised the power of gratitude, and now when I reflect on my life, it's like the universe has rewarded me. I literally wake up every morning and say "thank you so much", and I genuinely mean it.

A Traditional Wedding / Honeymoon

With regard to our wedding, we initially set the date for late January, thinking a summer wedding on the Mornington Peninsula would be lovely; however, the universe had other plans as it turned out and we couldn't get married at that time due to some legal complications. After taking a few deep breaths and remaining philosophical, we reset the date for Saturday 6 May to be held in our home town of Melbourne.

When I got married the first time, it was a very small affair with a marriage celebrant to perform the ceremony, and then on to enjoy a lovely intimate luncheon at a beautiful and very prestigious restaurant. It was a nice afternoon shared with close family members and two friends; however, it certainly was not a "traditional" wedding.

This time around, we both decided to share a fairly traditional wedding, again with a marriage celebrant for the ceremony. It was extremely important to my husband that we celebrate with our close family and friends, so we organised a lovely wedding at an Art Deco boutique hotel on the outskirts of the city. The venue was amazing and everything from our perspective was perfect. It was truly great to get many of our loved ones together to witness the start of our formal commitment.

Our 14-day honeymoon to Singapore and Thailand was fabulous, and included great accommodation, great food, shopping, and we combined this with sightseeing and lots of relaxation. Afterwards it was back home to begin our lives as Mr. and Mrs. Worthy.

Travelling the World Together

In 2018, my husband and I planned our dream trip, which entailed five weeks in Europe, travelling to quite a few different countries and involved a lot of touring and sightseeing. We visited Paris, London, Italy (Rome & Florence) and then on to Budapest to board a river cruise to Amsterdam. Vienna and Bratislava were absolute highlights, as was attending the Opera in both Florence and Vienna, which was also incredible.

These adventures were absolutely spectacular, with life-long, wonderful memories created by our dream trip. We were even so fortunate to meet some other awesome Aussies on the river cruise, and have now made some life-long friendships.

As soon as we returned home we booked our next holiday to Bali in January (2019). This holiday was a very different one in that it was far more relaxing. I also utilised this time in Bali to work on my business as the creative juices I seem to get whilst in Bali are quite incredible.

I think Bali can certainly be one of those relaxation holidays where you lie in the sun, by the pool, eat, read, write and sleep. Adding to the mix a lot of self-care with beauty treatments, massages, facials, rose baths and eating healthy and nutritious food, it is definitely my favourite destination.

I now visit Bali at least three to four times per year. It's always blissful and such a magnificent place for healing. I cannot think of a better location to mix business with pleasure. In addition, it's a place where you can be pampered every single day.

For both my husband I are so travelling and freedom have become such aligned values. We both feel deeply that travelling the world and experiencing different cultures, languages, food and history is one our greatest joys. I love that we can enjoy wonderful holidays together, or I can alternatively go solo on some adventures.

I also feel truly blessed that I have created such a magnificent life, with and without my Mr Worthy. I feel very blessed that we do not always have to spend every moment together, including having some holiday's and / or adventures without each other.

There are times when we quite happily travel on our own to various destinations to do our "work". I really enjoy my "me" time as well as my time with my husband, and I feel that the balance of the two has really helped me to feel even happier and more balanced. This is also a great indication that I do not rely on my husband for my entire source of my happiness, which was a pattern that I thankfully changed. My husband provides a lot of a happiness to me and I am so grateful for our wonderful times that we share together, but I have become accountable for designing my individual life and creating "individual" happiness within

Commitment

I am a woman who experienced so much loss, betrayal, and heartbreak, and didn't know whether I would get married again, or whether or not I really wanted to. For most of my life, I had fears around marriage, and then my first disastrous marriage only deepened my fears.

Now, here I am, mostly loving being married to my wonderful man. Of course, no marriage is perfect and there is ongoing work to be done and challenges to overcome. The point is though, I have so much joy in my heart and I want to encourage others to never give up on love, regardless of any heartbreaks or traumas they might have experienced in their past. **You can change, your life can change, you can forgive, heal, and you can and will fall in love once again, if that is your true desire.**

Your Path to Commitment

Our paths to commitment can be difficult, as we navigate our past suffering, loss and betrayal. Many women can become serial relationship rejecters as well, going from one relationship to the next, or alternatively never choosing to have a relationship and going to great lengths to avoid them.

The first key component to establishing commitment is allowing yourself to fully commit to yourself. This means **loving you, respecting you, valuing you and honouring you.** As mentioned, I really believe once you achieve this you can fully commit to another person, and in turn form an amazing relationship.

I believe the key elements to a successful and committed relationship are:

- *Sharing and compromise.*
- *Open communication that is loving and real.*
- *Allowing space for one another – having your own interests/friendships and time for self.*
- *Holding space for one another without argument, interruptions or shutting each other out – engaging without distractions of television, phones, computers etc.*
- *Regular intimacy/touch.*
- *Supporting each other's values and dreams.*
- *Having fun and experiencing life's adventures.*

In our relationships, we want to be loved, supported and heard, and we want a genuine respectful relationship, otherwise why bother? We may as well be on our own, rather than put up with a second-rate relationship, where dreams and values are not shared and you are not loved, adored and respected.

My husband and I worked through a lot of our **children's issues** and, thank goodness, we were able to still love and support our children but at the same time be able to **stand by each other**. There were challenges and conflicts and at times we were manipulated and caught in the middle of our children and their wants, needs and indeed fears.

In many instances, children can be the cause of relationships breaking down, especially when dealing with blended families and the different values or ways they have been brought up. You need to put every effort into making your relationship work, and do not allow the children to manipulate you or your relationship.

You may have to take off the "blinkers", as sometimes you do not see clearly how manipulative children can be. You need to reassure them that your love for them will never change, but at the same time remind them that you have a new relationship and you love your partner as well. You can still make time for them and make effort to spend 1:1 time so they do not feel ignored.

You are entitled to a life outside of the children and this can be a big transition and a new way of life for them, particularly if you have given them so much time and attention prior to your new love coming onto the scene. Children (adult children included) just want to know they are loved, and you need to reassure them, but at the same time set clear boundaries and be mindful of unacceptable behaviour.

Communication

As a couple, it's exceptionally important that you **communicate clearly and openly.** I believe this can resolve a lot of relationship problems before they become too serious. It's also about how you communicate, including the tone of your voice and your body language. It's great to have open communication; however, it's not good if you are yelling at each other and being mean to one another.

If you find that you are starting to get abusive in any way, you need to address that issue, as any form of verbal abuse can be soul destroying, and it should never be tolerated. It can be a pattern that some couples adopt, particularly if they are stressed or witnessed this type of behaviour with their own parents and/or upbringing.

My philosophy in my relationship is to always try to be kind and considerate to one another. Being stressed is not an excuse to treat one of the most important people in your life poorly. Be patient and kind as your first response, and if you are starting to yell and become angry at things that are not that significant, realise this is a sign that you need to find better ways of dealing with your stress.

If you find that your partner is starting to become verbally abusive in their communication, please do not accept this form of behaviour, and call attention to it immediately. You want to set clear boundaries that this behaviour is not acceptable. Do not become verbally abusive yourself, as this will just turn your relationship very toxic very quickly.

Find that courage within, to gently tell your partner it's not acceptable behaviour, and could they please try and communicate to you in a more loving way. If they don't listen, they may need to work out why they are being so "triggered", by taking their frustrations out on you, to try to understand why they are being abusive in the first place.

Of course, **there is no relationship that is perfect,** although it's vital that you are able to **talk about your issues and stay connected**. Being **loving and respectful** of each other, and not taking out your own personal stresses on each other, really helps the relationship to stay peaceful.

As a couple, we also **learn to say sorry to each other and not be too proud to admit our mistakes or our bad behaviour.** There may be occasions where you get a bit heated and say the wrong thing and in the wrong way, but it's important that you admit to your bad behaviour and apologise.

This does not mean that you can continue to be abusive or accept abuse because you lost your temper or your partner lost theirs, where things were said in the heat of the moment. This should not become normalized behaviour and an apology needs to be given. "I'm sorry" are two very powerful words. The apology needs to be genuine and other methods of dealing with stress are clearly required.

I also believe if your parents argued and/or were abusive, as a result you may share some negative conditioning that you need to release, as you may have unconsciously adopted some of their behaviours.

It is vitally important to make time **for intimacy as well, in all forms, from kissing, or holding hands to cuddling on the couch. In my view it cannot be just about sexual intimacy; however, that's also very important.** I know that it can be very easy to become complacent, and the reality is we are often too tired, and the last thing on our mind is sex, so we avoid any form of intimacy. However, in our busy stressed lives, there is a need to make time for sex as well, and certainly touch, which I believe should be a daily occurrence.

Another key learning is that unless we're healed from our pain, we will often attract someone who is also dealing with their own suffering and insecurities, and brings their own "baggage" to the relationship if they have not healed. If you are both **willing** to work on it individually, and then together as a couple, then it won't become a huge issue as, realistically, we are always working on some level of healing and growing. It will depend on the severity of what needs to be healed as to whether it is going to detrimentally impact your relationship.

It's also wise to reflect back on your life and assess whether you have been attracting lost souls, and if your natural state is being the "rescuer", or maybe it is you who in fact wants to be rescued. You need to realise that the only person who can rescue you is yourself, and this was one of my harshest lessons. **Don't think that you can "rescue" others, and do not expect others to "rescue" you.**

Don't go looking outside of yourself, you need to do your work, be accountable, forgive at a deep level, be open to the healing, release your fears and then you can fully commit to another person. Prior to this we are walking on what I would describe as "dangerous territory", where an "explosion" is potentially waiting to happen. Once you do the work and allow yourself to heal deeply, I do believe your vibration will change and you will attract someone with a similar frequency.

The biggest learning here is that you need to be accountable, and to put the work in on yourself to address any triggers and/or unresolved pain and trauma from your past. As a couple, you will need to stop projecting your deep-seated past pains onto each other, as I suspect this is what will happen if you have not both dealt with your previous suffering. Projecting is a huge indication that further healing is required to prevent this from continuing.

In summary, **heal yourself, do your work, save yourself, and don't expect anyone else to do it for you**. Others can help you on your journey, but you have to be the one to change, to want to improve yourself and allow love in so you can commit, fully. The key is to commit to yourself first before you commit yourself to another.

Travelling Together

I highly recommend that as a couple you experience different parts of the world together. Of course, you can still travel separately either as a solo traveller or with friends, however being able to travel with the person that you love is an incredible experience to share together. Creating life-long memories you can both regularly talk about will create more "juice" within the relationship.

Travelling together is also a great way to get out of the rut and routine of your "normal" life, which is also great for your relationship. It keeps life interesting, and planning your next holiday together is exciting. In addition, it can be a great motivator to continue to work hard so you can save towards a shared goal, which is very fulfilling.

If you are someone who hasn't travelled a lot, I have to warn you, (and I'm sure anyone who has travelled extensively will say the same thing), that the "travel bug" is contagious and should not be underestimated. Whether you are travelling with your partner, friends, family or as a solo-traveller, it will enrich your life in so many ways. The freedom to travel has certainly become one of my highest values. If it is also one of your values, make sure that you are making plans to travel and make it happen. Travel is now a big component of creating a "deliciously divine" life for myself.

Key Lessons:

If you are NOT in a relationship:

- ❖ Allow yourself to accept a loving committed relationship.
- ❖ Know that you can heal from your previous losses and grief.
- ❖ Start to affirm and visualise a wonderful relationship once again.
- ❖ Do not expect to be rescued or be the rescuer when you do form a relationship.
- ❖ Know that you are worthy of commitment.
- ❖ Continue to lead a juicy life with travel, creativity and great friends, until you meet someone who you are compatible with.

If you are in a relationship:

- Maintain open and loving communication.
- Maintain respect towards your partner and be kind and loving toward each other.
- Always be honest, have integrity and be respectful.
- Stick to your values system and boundaries, and communicate these in a loving and assertive way – voice your truth.
- Be each other's best friend – have each other's back at all times.
- Be intimate with one another, openly showing affection, not just when having sex.
- Have regular sexual intimacy and sensual play.
- Tell each other frequently that you love and adore them.
- Share adventures together and travel the world.
- Never be complacent and appreciate each other.
- Laugh together – maintain your sense of humour.
- Have mutual things in common but also share your own individual passions.
- Maintain your own friendships – you need your girlfriend time as well.
- Do not devote your entire life to your partner, maintain your friendships, have your own career/business/job, your own financial independence, your own interests (as well as shared ones).

You need to know that you deserve:

- *A companion who you can travel with, have dinners with, share your inner-felt secrets and desires with.*

- ❖ *Regular sex and intimacy. Women of any age can enjoy a loving and intimate relationship.*
- ❖ *To fall in love once again and know that you can create a committed, loving, and respectful relationship.*

"Stop letting your fear condemn you to mediocrity"

– Steve Maraboli

Lesson 20

You Are Worthy of Magnificence

My journey to create my magnificent life has at times been intense and challenging, and there has been a lot of suffering to overcome. I have had many harsh lessons to learn, and on many occasions unfortunately I did it the hard way. There were many instances where I felt alone, disconnected, a failure, and at times even completely worthless, leading a very mediocre existence. It's only over the last few years that I have been able to say that my life is now "deliciously divine".

To reach this stage in my life where I allow my own light to shine brightly, to honour, support, and know my own worth, is truly extraordinary. I am genuinely so grateful and appreciative and will endeavour to never take my life for granted. Every day I feel blessed and grateful that I can awake with excitement and enthusiasm; excited for the adventures that lie ahead of me, and knowing that the opportunities available to me are endless.

Compared to my past, there are very few days when I wake up wondering how I am going to get through the day, struggling, exhausted and not feeling excited about my life. I finally made that firm agreement with myself, no matter what my lessons were, I would learn them, grow, expand and live the life I know that I deserve, and one that is truly "magnificent".

There were periods in my life where I momentarily doubted if it was possible to truly lead a magnificent life. Luckily, there was something deep down inside of me, even at my lowest, that knew I could change and I did not have to keep suffering and accepting mediocrity.

From Ordinary to Extraordinary

Through my huge journey of self-development and lesson learning, I have discovered a strong calling to help other women to take their lives from ordinary to extraordinary. The main reason I continued to write this book was to primarily help you understand and recognise how worthy of love you are.

You do not need to keep suffering, you do not need to continue to be a victim of your past, and you are just as deserving as anyone else in the world to truly create the life that you want. The kind of life that you live on your terms.

As you can understand from reading my story, time after time I settled in my life many times as I attracted many mediocre, bad or plain toxic relationships, and I made very lousy career choices. The great news is that there is a better path to take, and that you can make more informed choices and ones that are for your highest good. You do not have to keep suffering, and you do not have to go through all these extremely painful lessons alone. You can become completely conscious of your life and then put together a plan to improve it.

You can start right now creating your very own masterpiece, and you need to realise and feel deep down in your own heart and soul that you are completely deserving. It's part of your soul's journey and the universe is waiting for you to open your arms and accept all the magnificence that you desire. It's now time to appreciate all that you have received and all that you will receive.

Your Path to Magnificence

Celebrate Your Life

My belief is that your life is worth celebrating every day, not just on special occasions. I think it is unfortunate that there are people I meet who do not even celebrate their own birthday. This saddens me that people cannot even celebrate their own lives.

Many are fearful of getting older, and don't want to be reminded of their age, which is a terrible excuse. After all, age is just a number, and what comes with age is an innate wisdom and understanding that can never be underestimated. We all need to embrace whatever age we are, make the best of what we have and celebrate our lives. Never live with regrets, and do everything you can to live with peace and joy in your heart.

I recommend that you stop and take a breath and think about some of the things that you can celebrate about yourself today. Provide a reward to yourself. Buy yourself those flowers, go and have that massage, or buy that glass of your favourite champagne. What are you waiting for? The time to value and appreciate yourself is now.

To me life can either be one big celebration or one big misery. What will you choose?

Life is Too Short for Bad Anything

Do not leave the "special" items for a special day, as every day is special. Use your best china, cutlery, crystal, wear the good underwear, eat the best food and the very best of everything that is within your budget. Your life is special every single day and you need to start living like it is. Truly believe how blessed you are, concentrate on everything that you do have, never obsessing over what you don't have.

Do Not Settle

Whether it be in your career, business or job, your relationships or friendships, etc., know that you deserve magnificence in all areas of your life. Know that you do not have to accept mediocrity – it does not have to be a continued habit. If it is a habit then start to change your habits for the better, and know you can change regardless of your past.

Please do not settle in a relationship, because you feel lonely and you crave connection, as it will most likely not be a very healthy relationship. **Make an agreement with yourself and know you are worth great relationships and friendships. Accept nothing less than that.**

Have a Travel Fund

You should **have a travel fund and travel as much as possible.** It took me until my late 30's before I went overseas, to Hawaii, and it was an amazing experience. This really opened my eyes to the possibility of new adventures, and how wonderful it was to be able to travel to foreign lands. If you really want to travel, make sure you create a "travel fund" and put money away every single week to save for your next trip. This practice is setting a clear intention so you can manifest what you desire.

Even if it starts as a small amount, you have set the intention and have opened the energy to allow you to achieve this dream. I have found that spending my income on experiences and personal development, as well as investing in my business, are the most fulfilling investments, rather than just buying unnecessary "stuff".

Daily Self Care is essential

Self-care is something that should be a daily habit, not just something we undertake when at retreats. I believe that looking after yourself and making yourself a priority is a "not negotiable". Even if it's only for 15 minutes a day, it can make a difference. You need to understand that you are worth at least that much time to concentrate on you. Also, once you "fill your own cup", you can then fill others, however if you are exhausted, grumpy and resentful, then you will not be able to give to others in a positive and inspiring way.

Create an abundant mentality

Don't be a 'scrooge' with your money, and don't think that after you pay your bills that you have to save every penny and live a life in lack. Believe me I have witnessed this plenty of times in my life. It's great to have a steady and stable savings plan, however I do not recommend that you completely deny yourself of actually living a life. It's great if you splurge from time to time on some luxuries - it's a great way to reward yourself and display a more abundant mentality.

Vision Boards & Journals are Powerful

Vision boards and journals are exceptionally valuable tools in assisting you to create your magnificent life. I suggest that prior to starting the process of creating a vision board and/or book, that you meditate before you start the process. Ask yourself these questions, and as you answer these questions in your mind, visualise your response very clearly:

- ❖ *Where do I want to live?*
- ❖ *What type of relationship do I want?*
- ❖ *What types of friendships do I want?*
- ❖ *What type of work do I want to be doing?*
- ❖ *Where do I want to travel to?*
- ❖ *How do I want to feel?*
- ❖ *How do I want to look?*

As you are answering these questions and visualising, actually:

***Smell it ~ Feel it ~ Taste it ~ See it ~ Create it
Embody the Whole Experience***

You can get as creative as you like with this project, and there are many variations as to how you can implement this. The traditional way is to go and get yourself a blank canvas board, have a great selection of magazines, glue and scissors. Once you start flicking through the magazines, cut out any images that align with your vision.

You can then create a collage on your blank canvas, and start cutting and pasting. You can add words, images, or anything that is in alignment with your vision. It's actually a very therapeutic and meditative process, and when I host my own workshops, I love to surround my home with a combination of flowers, oils and relaxation music to set the whole mood to create a healing sanctuary.

Personally, I prefer keeping a "joy list" in my vision journal and as the year progresses, I cut out sayings, write new affirmations, and I add new content as my ideas expand and my vision changes and/or becomes clearer. I also set aside regular times where I mediate and visualise my "deliciously divine" life, and then write my insights into my journal. I recommend that you try this for yourself by keep your own "joy list" and add to it regularly, making sure you are doing the things listed on your list consistently and update your journal as the year progresses.

***Have a clear vision of what you want to achieve and stay on
your path until you achieve it***

Affirmations

Once you have a clear vision of what you want to create in your life, you can start designing affirmations for exactly what you want to create. Always start your affirmation with "I am", as this is so much more powerful.

Create your own affirmations and post them in a place where you will see them every day, keep repeating them whilst also visualizing your vision. At the same time, be very clear on what you want in your life, and really start believing you can create it. The number one reason why visualisations and affirmations don't work, is because part of you is not believing, the second reason is you're not putting in the action is required for your dreams to be materialised.

Make your life a priority no matter what your circumstances are, which includes gender, socioeconomic position, family, friends, ex-boyfriends, and husbands. Make the decision that you will create the best version of YOU, and you will create the best life possible for yourself. You are the master of your destiny and it's no one else's responsibility to create your happiness and your magnificent life.

Make Yourself a Priority

Think about some of the times in your life where you may have just settled. Was it in your relationships? Your career? Your friendships? Once you recognise that you have been settling in your own life, you can then start the process of making the changes to help you create far more happiness and a life that is "juicy".

The universe will also help you to reach where you want to be if you are being very clear and precise about your goals. This won't happen automatically, and you actually do need to do the work first and not just wait for a miracle to occur. As I have stated previously, if you are unclear, the universe will be unclear too, so make sure you are very specific and not wishy-washy with your desires.

Be crystal clear with what you want so the universe knows how to help you create your deepest desires

Be Open to Change

It's time to stop complaining about your life and listen to what you are constantly complaining about. When you really listen, you will realise very quickly the things you need to change, and you can then put an action plan in place.

Your life is extremely important and precious so make the effort and put the necessary action in so that your life aligns with what you want. If you don't make the effort in your own life, how do you expect others to make the effort with you? What you feel you attract, what you think you attract, so be really mindful of your thoughts and what you feel, so that you can adapt your language and change your mindset accordingly.

Ban the Negative Self-Talk

What lies are you continuing to tell yourself? Are you saying that you are not good enough? Smart enough? Attractive enough? If you are, it's really time to ban this negative self-talk, as it will not serve you in anyway. Stop the BS and call yourself out on the lies you are telling yourself — some of which you have probably been repeating for years. This type of communication style will keep you small, and prevent you from living the best life possible.

It can take some practice but in time you will naturally speak positively about yourself, and eventually stop the self-doubt and limiting thought patterns. A great start would be for every time you say or think something negative about yourself, stop and replace it with something more positive and uplifting.

Accept Compliments

How often do we reject a compliment? How often do we just brush it off or reduce it in some way? Train yourself to smile and thank the person giving it to you. When you receive a compliment, feel it, embody it, and really appreciate the person who has complimented you. Feel proud that you have been complimented and accept it in its full glory.

Key Lessons:

- ❖ Do not settle for a mediocre life, it's your birthright to claim magnificence.
- ❖ Take your power back now and lead from your heart and soul.
- ❖ Be honest with yourself with regard to where you can make improvements.
- ❖ Stop doubting yourself and start believing.
- ❖ Love yourself a little more each day.
- ❖ Do not compete or compare yourself to others, as you are on your own path and you are unique. No one has what you have.
- ❖ Value your life and value yourself.
- ❖ Know that you are just as deserving as anyone else to create magnificence.
- ❖ Have strong boundaries – do not put up with being treated badly or disrespectfully.
- ❖ Know what you want in your life and what you do not want.
- ❖ Have enormous gratitude for every wonderful person.
- ❖ Realise that you mind is so powerful, be careful what you think and say.
- ❖ Be generous, be compassionate, be the VERY BEST VERSION OF YOU.

- ❖ The only person you need to worry about whether or not they like you, is YOU.
- ❖ Be true to who you are and what you stand for.
- ❖ Stop wasting energy on whether people like you — LIKE yourself and others are more likely to.

Dear MAGNIFICENT woman

Do you know that you are beautiful beyond measure?
That you are unique and that you are worthy of magnificence?
It's time for you to once and for all start believing this and feel it deeply within your heart & soul.
It's time for you now to finally give yourself permission to heal your wounds from the past, letting go of the disappointments and betrayals that you have held onto, preventing you from being the very best version that you can be.
It's time to trust yourself once again and open your heart fully.
It's time to love yourself a little more each day so you can allow more MAGNIFICENCE to be created. I want your life to become more enriched and more abundant, as that is what you DESERVE.
It's time to embrace all that you are, your light, your shadow,
And know that you are imperfectly perfect.
It's time to allow yourself to be that amazing woman that you are destined to be, and allow the universe to provide for you with your true desires whilst you consciously create the life that you have dreamed of and have clearly visualised.
Be kind, compassionate and loving, yet remain strong in your convictions, and keep on track regardless of other people's opinions.
Be brave beautiful woman and do not allow fear to paralyse you from achieving everything you desire.

The universe is waiting for you to step up and be that woman you were destined to be.

You were born to be MAGNIFICENT and sprinkle your "Magic" everywhere you go.

Be bold, be brave and shine your brilliance, be visible and even when your fears are real, do it scared regardless.

Make it your mission to live with passion, purpose and dedication, allowing yourself to truly love and adore who you are, what you offer and what your stand for, as this is where your true inner and outer beauty will shine naturally,

creating your very own masterpiece and allowing you to embody every

part of your MAGNIFCENCE.

YOU ARE MAGNIFICENT!

Jo Worthy

"All our dreams can come true if we have the courage to pursue them"

– Walt Disney

Lesson 21

You Are Worthy of Dreams Coming True

My life's journey has been a huge one with many challenges overcome, and I realise how far I have progressed. My life these days is a very different story from my life as an insecure fearful child, the one I had as a teenager who rejected love and had nervous breakdowns, and the one where I was a woman who attracted three toxic and abusive relationships.

Similarly, it is very different from when I numbed out my pain with addictions of gambling and to a lesser extent, food, sex and shopping. My life now is so amazingly different and so much juicier, and many of my dreams have come true.

In true Scorpio style, I have completely transformed my life in so many ways. The biggest lesson and advice that I could give anyone is: **when you learn to love, honour and respect yourself, huge transformations can happen to you.** Your own dreams can become a reality.

I learned to back myself, to stop the negative self-talk, conditioning and patterns that were severely affecting my life. You can do this as well. I learned to create solid healthy boundaries, and the art of self-care, self-love and self-respect — to the point where my dreams started to be realised and the "miracles" occurred.

The moment I said enough is enough, and understood I was deserving of a much happier existence, was when I took back my power and connected to my courage. I eliminated the harsh criticisms of self, the judgments and negative self-talk, the feelings and behaviours that kept me small and prevented me from being the very best version of myself. This was when everything began to change in such incredible ways. The day that I decided to dig deeper and heal, forgive and release the shame, guilt, and the harsh judgments on my myself, **was when my life did start to feel like my dreams were being realised.**

I am not going to sugar-coat my life and say that it wasn't tough to get to the point where I am now. My journey was challenging and the road that I travelled was very rocky and even dangerous at times. There were many instances where I felt I just wanted to give up and take an easier route. I would "drive" forward, and then it seemed I would take another route and end up further behind on my journey.

I went off my route many times and landed in many "pot holes". I came across many "road blocks", and steep mountains to drive-up, plus there were huge moments of FEAR where I wanted to turn around, even when parts of me knew this was the journey that would change everything.

There were many moments of thinking I couldn't do this any longer. I thought: this road is too long, too bumpy and just too exhausting. I wanted to stop this journey, and wanted an easier road that was smoother, and with less hazards everywhere. It was only when I surrendered to heal and change, and when I finally thought more highly of myself that the road would become a lot smoother.

It was when in my 40's that real "miracles" occurred and where my warrior woman kicked in and I connected to the goddess within me. This is the energy that we call ALL connect to. It was then that I decided I would finish this journey but realising it didn't have been so challenging and painful. I knew that I had to keep persevering to improve my life and that I needed to commit to ME and that I would make every effort possible to be the absolute BEST that I could be.

A summary of the "reminders" to self:

- ❖ *Dig deeper to heal even more.*
- ❖ *Forgive myself and release all that shame and guilt that I had carried around for years.*
- ❖ *Love me and back me and discover that I could even fall in love again.*
- ❖ *Give me a deep realisation that we were all born amazing and magnificent, we just needed to connect to it.*

It was then that I decided to upgrade my "vehicle" so that I could be the very best version of me. It also became evident that I was going to enjoy so much more beauty, and know I deserved so much more "comfort". Upgrading to a better "vehicle" was reward for not taking the easy route, for not just driving back to my comfort zone and not changing direction. The universe was rewarding me, as I was also rewarding myself.

Was this another big part of the puzzle that I had just discovered? Was this the answer to my dreams? Once I decided I would only settle for the best option, the best "vehicle", and that I was worth it and deserving, I would then be rewarded with joy, peace, harmony and, most importantly, more LOVE.

Connecting to my own "super powers" has allowed me to start to build a truly inspiring and fabulous life. I have so much to be thankful for, and more importantly, I am so grateful I didn't give up on me! I am proud I was resilient and didn't allow my past to keep me stuck, and I kept going until I broke down the insecurities, the fears and decided to accept, respect and honour me.

Now, I feel I am actually living, not just walking around half dead and accepting mediocrity. I am at a stage of my life where I don't just go through the motions of life, of eating, sleeping, going to work, rinse and repeat. Instead, I get up in the morning, am excited, feel love and joy in my heart and soul, and most days I can't wait to start my day.

I have connected to my passions of writing, creating communities, and travelling the world. The best realisation was that I do not need to live a life of instability, uncertainty, and to be driven by FEAR.

Your Path to Creating Your Dreams

Throughout this book I have shared quite a lot of tools to help you create a magnificent life. I honestly believe we can all create a path that will bring our dreams into our current reality, and you too can live "the dream". You need to be clear about what your dreams are, and then start to visualise, plan and then put in the required ACTION.

Action Steps for creating an amazing life:

- Introduce more joy into your life by creating a life that you love – refer to your "joy list" often.
- Make the power of gratitude a daily habit.
- Continue the journey of improving your self-love and making yourself a priority.
- Practice forgiveness regularly.
- Release your fear or "do it scared regardless".
- Connect with your genius/your gifts and use them to not only bring you more joy, but also to help others as well.
- Utilise your creative talents – this will be unique to you.
- Your pain is often your purpose – teach others what you have learnt and how you have transformed.
- Practice the power formula of affirmations, visualisations, beliefs and actions.

Planning:

In combination with all the visualisations and affirmations I have recommended, you also need to incorporate the practical approach to really help your dreams come true. Planning is something that is an essential ingredient to your success and your dreams coming to fruition.

"If you fail to plan, you are planning to fail"
Benjamin Franklin

You want to set yourself up for success - not failure, so some form of planning is required.

Do you currently have daily, weekly, monthly and yearly goals? The visualisations and affirmations recommended throughout this book are great, but you also need to take the necessary **action** in combination with some practical tools. You may become very disappointed with your results if you have not planned and put in the effort for action. Even a simple list of your priorities for each day/week will help you to keep on target.

There are many ways you can implement a plan. For example, you can use wall planners, diaries, or weekly planners on your desk, and write out "to do" lists. Find out what suits you, plan your life, and make it your mission to create your life on your terms.

Loving you, believing in you, and connecting to your brilliance, your magnificence is when your dreams can come true. You are worthy of this.

Suggestions to get the "think tank" into action:

What would you love to do in your life that you haven't done or achieved? Do you want a degree in a particular field? Do you want to completely change your career direction? Start to really think about it and write down all the things that you would like to do — things that you haven't as yet done in your life.

Do you want to invest more in your personal development? Complete training courses that will not only expand your knowledge, but provide you with new skills? Read books that inspire you? Be around other like-minded people that help inspire you to be the best version of you?

What are your gifts and talents? Are you utilising these? Are you allowing yourself the right to shine in your particular area of expertise? If you can't create a career based on your desires, make sure you are bringing some of the things that *light you up* into your life.

My personal example, was my passion for performing and writing as a young child, but then I stopped doing those things. Although I did not go into a career in the arts, as a young adult I did join a local amateur theatre company and also studied performance and theatre at TAFE.

Later in life I found my love for writing returned, which led me to write this book, which is a big achievement. If you have a burning desire to do something that you haven't done yet, or you once loved to do, add it to your list and make it a mission to tick it off your list.

Once you have your list, start to break it down into smaller components. For me, I love using post-it notes, creating a simple three column formula of To Do, WIP (Work in Progress), and Done.

I find the built-in cupboards in my home office are ideal to create this type of "board". All you need are some coloured post-it notes and Sharpie Permanent Markers, to create your planning board. I love this concept, because it's not only visual, but it's active. You can easily move the post-it notes around, allowing you to update your "board" very easily.

> *CREATE a plan, put in the required ACTION, stay focussed and do not stop until you reach your TARGET.*

It's time to fall in love with YOU

Dear beautiful one

It's time to stop the worry about what

everyone else is thinking and doing

It's time to stop worrying if others are judging you

It's time to honour all of you and your beautiful essence

Of who you are and what you stand for

It's time to appreciate all of you

It's time to shine your amazingness

It's time from this day forward to make

the necessary changes so you can be

The very best version of YOU

It's time to give up the struggle

It's time to get rid of "Oh I am not good enough,

Smart enough, Pretty enough"

It's time to release the lies that we tell ourselves

It's time to trust YOU

It's time to forgive YOU

It's time to allow yourself to HEAL

It's time to celebrate all you have become

Your strength, your resilience and your vulnerabilities

It's time to be fully accountable for your life

It's time for you to step forward and take a bow

It's time to realise just how magnificent you truly are

It's time for you blossom like a gorgeous rose

It's time to embrace all of your layers and all of your

Unique beauty

Its time

To fall in LOVE with YOU

LOVE your life

It's time as your heart and soul are waiting

And cheering you on

It's YOUR time to love you more and be the best

version of you

It's time to be LOVE WORTHY

Jo Worthy

Conclusion

The most important advice I can give to you is to invest completely in becoming the best version of yourself. Any of the work that you undertake in improving yourself and your life, is without a doubt, worth every bit of your time and money, and I believe, will be one of your best investments.

This is your life, not someone else's to design. If you take total control and steer it in the direction that you want to go, knowing exactly what you want and keep your focus, you can achieve all that you desire.

Realise that you can create the life that you love and your deepest desires can be fulfilled, regardless of what has happened in your past or what is happening right now, in your present. Know deep down in your heart that your future can be amazing once you:

- ❖ *Change your mindset.*
- ❖ *Heal from your past hurts.*
- ❖ *Forgive yourself.*
- ❖ *Create peace in your heart and soul.*
- ❖ *Respect, honour and fall in love with YOU.*

Some of my lessons I know have been harsh. However, through all the dark days that I experienced, I eventually got to experience a life filled with so much beautiful light.

My experiences have given me much wisdom, which has led me to share my story. More importantly, had I not shared it, I would be doing a great injustice to all women who might need to hear my story to enable them to find inspiration within their own lives. Bad things can happen to good people when we are not aligned with our purpose, live in FEAR, do not create healthy boundaries and do not protect our own energy.

After reading my story, realise that regardless of all the adversity I experienced, I could still reinvent myself and transform. Even when I hit rock bottom, quite a few times throughout my life, I didn't lose hope about the possibility of changing my life for the better. I just had to find my way, and be on the path of LOVE not constant fear.

I can honestly say I truly love my life and the people I allow into my inner sanctuary. I love my husband, and love how appropriate it is that I became Mrs Worthy. My whole life's journey has been about increasing my own self-worth, to then become "Worthy" in name and in life.

Please, whatever you do in your life, do not EVER give up on yourself and do everything in your power to connect to more love. Never stop believing in you, even when you are being challenged and your heart is sinking or you feel like your heart has been ripped out and you're at the depths of dismay. Believe in yourself, and that your life can change and you can change.

Also know that life goes in cycles, and when you're experiencing the shitty horrible times, remember the cycle will turn around, and that life will improve immensely. Trust the flow and believe the universe has your back and believes in YOU, surrender, forgive and allow the healing and of course BELIEVE IN YOU.

Dig deep and tap into the resilience that lays within, shake the shit off and know that you can rebuild your life. Don't dwell on the negative for too long, or blame others for your life, every single thing that happens is for a reason and a learning. Thank every single person for the lesson, regardless of how painful it may have been. Your own accountability is also a big key to creating a much better existence.

With every ounce of your whole being, go forth and create the life of your dreams and don't stop until you've reached your desired destination!

I truly hope you haven't encountered some of the difficult lessons I experienced. I hope you value your life and continue the search to become a better version of you. Raise your standards and don't accept second best. You deserve the greatest love of all – TO LOVE YOU FIRST and foremost.

You are worthy of CREATIVITY

You are worthy of being ADORED

You are worthy of PLEASURE

You are worthy of HEALING

You are worthy of LIVING PASSIONATLEY and ON PURPOSE

You are worthy of creating HEALTHY BOUNDARIES

You are worthy of OPULENCE

You are worthy of TRUTH

You are worthy of STABILITY

You are worthy of ABUNDANCE

You are worthy of BLISS

You are worthy of HARMONY

You are worthy of FINDING LOVE AGAIN

You are worthy of FRIENDSHIPS

You are worthy of COMMUNITY

You are worthy of SURRENDERING

You are worthy of UNCONDITIONAL LOVE

You are worthy of COMMITMENT

You are worthy of MAGNIFICENCE

You are WORTHY of your DREAMS COMING TRUE

I am sending much love, healing and peace, and may you live the life you have always imagined. Go forth and do not stop "painting" until you create your very own magnificent masterpiece.

You are Love Worthy Today, Tomorrow and Always

You need to know deep down in your heart & soul

You are worth it

You are more than worth it

You are more than enough

Now go forth and create the exact life that you have imagined and dreamt of

Do whatever it takes to live an amazing and beautiful life!

Acknowledgements

- My husband, who not only loves me with a full and devoted heart, but allows me to spread my wings and fly to be the best woman that I can be. He has accepted ALL of me: the great, the good, the bad and the sometimes ugly! My Mr Worthy, has been one of my biggest cheerleader and support as well as my best friend and confidant. He has loved and adored me, and has been my rock on numerous occasions. He has shown me what true love and commitment is, and that I am a "relationship type of woman".

- To my daughter, who amazes me with her intelligence, wisdom and beauty. I am so overjoyed that she has also started honouring herself as a woman and tapping into all her beautiful gifts and her creativity. She is such an adventurous woman and never allows fear to prevent her from doing what she wants to do.

  I am proud to be her mother and I hope I continue to inspire her and help her to never lose sight of her own magnificence. Words cannot do justice to the depth of love that I have for my daughter. It is pure, unconditional and eternal. Thankyou my beautiful girl for choosing me as your mother and for being such an absolute blessing in my life.

- To my Mum, Sylvia, who now lives with me in spirit and will always reside in my heart for eternity. I want to thank Mum from the bottom of my heart, for allowing me to indulge her with my creative writings and performing from the tender age of three. I thank her for her unconditional love she displayed throughout her entire life.

Life will never be the same without her, but I know she is around me, protecting, supporting me and hopefully proud of me for publishing this book and pursuing my dreams.

- To my loving and beautiful sister Debbie-Anne and her amazing daughter, (my niece) Elisse, for loving me, believing and supporting me. I deeply love these women and feel blessed they are not only my family, but such wonderful women as well. I appreciate you both and love you with all my heart. To my niece for also providing me with a great-niece, Heidi, who is so beautiful and blessed to have my niece and sister as their mother and grandmother.

- To my many mentors and coaches over my lifetime and a special thank you to Yvonne Teoh Bource who was an inspiration to me in my 30's and then we lost contact until a few years ago. I was so lucky to attend her transformational "connect to soul" retreat in Bali in 2018. Thankyou universe for your divine timing yet again!

- To Luanne Mareen who taught me about community, women's circles and leading a life on purpose. To all my other mentors, Susan Young, Ange De Lumiere, Rita Joyan, Pam Brossman, Jo Johnson, Blaise van Hecke & recently to Shaz Cino & Cathy Larter. For their guidance, wisdom, expertise and intuitive abilities as well – thank you. I have been so lucky to connect with all of these amazing souls!

- To my amazing and delightful artist/designer Emma Veiga-Malta from Bespoke Backdrops & Branding, who designed my gorgeous book cover which I adore. Emma has also created some exquisite, feminine and elegant new branding for me. Emma was a delight to work with and connected with my

Acknowledgements

vision and created a book cover that deeply represents growth, femininity and beauty and is very "Venus" inspired.

- I also want to thank my hypnotherapist Rick Morse (RIP) for helping me to heal another layer of sadness that lurked beneath the surface.

- To my "inner sanctuary" of friends who have given me faith and trust in female friendships and have loved and accepted me for all that I am. Huge gratitude and special thanks to Diana Russell, Val Pasquale, Sharyn Bailey, Sondre Callec & Sue Stott. You are all such a huge inspiration and I am blessed to know you, for some I also thank you for the lessons.

  You were available many times to provide love, support, encouragement, inspiration and your innate wisdom. I want you to know how much joy, love and happiness you have brought to me. I appreciate and thank you so much.

- Overall, I have had the absolute honour of meeting so many wonderful and talented women over the past few years including therapists, healers, artists, counsellors, massage therapists, reiki masters, and a whole collective of "juicy" and magnificent women who help me to become a better version of me as well, including connecting to my own intuitive powers.

  A special thanks to all the other array of wonderful wise and inspiring women, who have inspired and even challenged me over the past few years. I thank you all for being an integral part of my journey and growth as a woman.

- To the community of beautiful women who I adore and appreciate and I have had the privilege of working with over the past few years. I want to sincerely thank you for either loving me, supporting or teaching me so much. To any other woman who has supported me and brought joy, I am so thankful that you have been part of my life.

To my wonderful community I have had the honour and privilege of working with, particularly in Canberra and Melbourne. You have all played a part in knowing that I can make a difference and help transform other women's lives as well. It has brought me absolute joy to be able to touch your lives in some way, and I hope I continue to be an inspiration and supportive guide for you.

- A huge thank you to the publishers, cover designers, editors and proof readers. A massive thank you to Emily Gowor and Rae Antony from Gowor Publishing who showed me so much heart and soul in everything they do. A huge thank you for their advice on my front cover and the overall structure of this book. I also thank the editors, printers, layout designers and anyone else who assisted behind the scenes in getting this book published.

- I want to especially thank my friend Liese Ho for offering to look over my manuscript when I was visiting Bali recently. Liese did such a stellar job and really made this book a much better read. Liese has a true gift for editing with her laser eye and focus and I highly recommend her editing expertise.

- I have so much gratitude for you darling Liese and I thank you for your wisdom, honesty and also for the universe for such divine timing connecting with you.

- A special HUGE thank you to you as the reader! Thank you for allowing me to share my story with you. I sincerely hope I can help inspire you to create your own magnificent and "deliciously divine" life.

About The Author

Jo Worthy is an inspirational author, intuitive guide and also known as the "self-love" goddess. Jo is becoming well known in the personal development space within Australia and her true desire is to help women connect to their own power deep within so that they feel CONFIDENT, SEXY, VIBRANT AND DELICIOUS. Jo can support women on their journey of transformation and empowerment, helping them to HEAL, FORGIVE and LOVE with a pure open heart.

Jo has truly connected to her creativity and living a passionate and purposeful life. She is an inspirational leader in business and in the personal development sector. She is the host of women's retreats in Australia & Bali, and she conducts "magnificent you" virtual goddess gatherings through her membership group *Worthy Goddess Sanctuary*. Jo is in the process of creating some exciting new product, include an online program which outlines the main lessons within this book. This program will be called **"How to Create a Deliciously Divine LIfe - The Love, Abundance & Passion (LAP) online program.**

Jo is also a powerful intuitive and combines all her own superpowers to provide 1:1 soul mentoring to help, support and guide women on their journeys. Jo helps each woman to connect to their own magnificence so that they can lead more **vibrant, juicy and "deliciously divine**" lives.

Jo consciously started her personal development in her early 20's, realising early on in life the power of our minds and how we can create our reality. She has continued to search for deeper meaning and to improve her life to become a better version of herself. Jo realised that once she returned to these fundamentals, she could change her behaviour and indeed her life.

She has a corporate administration background and 30 years of personal development teachings, including the Law of Attraction and other modalities such as astrology. She has researched and studied extensively on the topic of women's empowerment, including the power of goddesses and has really developed her intuitive powers and combined with her practicality and her heart-felt authentic approach, her work has become transformational.

Jo is also an inspirational speaker and is presently available to bring her wisdom, experience and down to earth nature to any engagement, especially related to women's empowerment. Jo favourite keynotes are entitled *"How to create a deliciously divine life"and from "Mediocrity to Magnificence".* Although with Jo's vast life experience, she can customise her talks to suit any occasion. You can check out Jo's speaking profile on her website.

Jo was born in Melbourne, however now resides in Canberra, Australia with her husband and their beloved Burmese cat. Between them they have three adult children who reside in Melbourne, so the couple are now "empty-nesters". Jo's personal joy list includes writing, reading, personal development, women's empowerment, astrology, cooking, movies, music, retreating, travelling and connecting to other incredible and inspiring people – all these things make her heart sing and enable her to live a "deliciously divine" life.

Contact Jo at Jo@joworthy.com

www.Joworthy.com

Sales Page

Website: www.JoWorthy.Com
Facebook Business pages: joworthyloveworthy
Facebook Group: The Worthy Goddess Community
The Worthy Goddess Sanctuary (VIP Membership)
Instagram: joworthyinspirationalauthor

Jo offers the following services/products:

- 1:1 "magnificent you" consultations via Zoom
- Women's virtual circles – via her Worthy Goddess Sanctuary
- "Deliciously Divine" retreats for women held in Bali & Australia
- "How to live a Deliciously Divine Life" Love, Abundance & Passion (LAP) online program (to be launched in 2020)
- "You are Love Worthy" Affirmation Cards (to be launched in 2020)
- Love, Abundance & Passion Potions (to be launched in 2020)

Inspirational Speaking:

Signature talks include:

- From mediocrity to magnificence
- Living a passionate and purposeful life
- How to live a "deliciously divine" life

www.ingramcontent.com/pod-product-compliance
Lightning Source LLC
Chambersburg PA
CBHW062056290426
44110CB00022B/2612